YOGA
FOR CYCLISTS

YOGA FOR CYCLISTS

Lexie Williamson

BLOOMSBURY

LONDON · NEW DELHI · NEW YORK · SYDNEY

Note: While every effort has been made to ensure that the content of this book is as technically accurate and as sound as possible, neither the author nor the publishers can accept responsibility for any injury or loss sustained as a result of the use of this material.

Published by Bloomsbury Publishing Plc
50 Bedford Square
London WC1B 3DP
www.bloomsbury.com

Bloomsbury is a trademark of Bloomsbury Publishing Plc

First edition 2014

ISBN (print): 978-1-4081-904-7-0
ISBN (edpf): 978-1-4081-9064-7
ISBN (epub): 978-1-4081-9063-0

A CIP catalogue record for this book is available from the British Library.

Acknowledgements
Cover photograph © Getty Images
All inside images © John-Paul Bland Photography, www.jpbland.co.uk with the exception of the following: pp. 24, 63, 148, 169, 170 (top), 171, 173, 175, 176 and 181 © Shutterstock; p. 6 © Marchkimoo/Shutterstock.com; p. 8 © Wesseldu Plooy/Shutterstock.com; p.19 © Dawid Lech/Shutterstock.com; pp. 34, 37, 40, 47 and 164 © Rena Schild/Shutterstock.com; p. 36 © EcoPrint/Shutterstock.com; pp. 45, 48 and 172 x 2 © Radu Razvan/Shutterstock.com; p.168 © Maxim Pertichuk/Shutterstock.com; p. 177 © Ricardo Esplana Babor/Shutterstock.com; p.178 © Joe Ferrer/Shutterstock.com; pp. 110, 167 and 170 (bottom) © Getty Images

Commissioning Editor: Lisa Thomas
Editor: Sarah Cole
Design: Rod Teasdale

This book is produced using paper that is made from wood grown in managed, sustainable forests. It is natural, renewable and recyclable. The logging and manufacturing processes conform to the environmental regulations of the country of origin.

Typeset in 9.5pt on 13pt Myriad Pro Light by White Rabbit Editions, Barnstaple, Devon.
Printed and bound in China by C&C Offset Printing Co.
10 9 8 7 6 5 4 3 2

CONTENTS

ACKNOWLEDGEMENTS

I would like to thank the sports scientists Dr. Chris Edmundson and Dr. George Dallam, physiotherapist Ian Brocklesby, sports psychologist and cycling coach Alan Heary and Professor of Applied Physiology Alison McConnell for their valued contributions to this book. Thank you also to those who contributed quotes to *Yoga for Cyclists*. They are the cyclists Phil Sykes, Benjamin Chaddock, Kristen Gentilucci, and Nick Rice; physical therapist and former pro cyclist Ciarán Power and coach and author Thomas Chapple. I also extend my gratitude to the cyclists and triathletes who donated their precious time to model for this book. They are: Darren Moore, Layla Smith, Jimmy Wilson and Paul Winks. The photographer John-Paul Bland deserves a special mention for his patience and perfectionism. Last but not least, I would like to mention my fantastic, supportive family: Cameron, Finlay, Lauren Skye and husband, Tom.

PREFACE

Over the last ten years the number of athletes incorporating yoga into their training has grown dramatically. Andy Murray, Ryan Giggs and Jessica Ennis-Hill are high-profile examples of elite-level sportspeople who use yoga to stay supple, avoid injuries and prolong their careers. Many soccer, rugby and American football teams now have their own team yoga instructor on the payroll.

But athletes who take up yoga to stay injury-free often also discover an additional range of performance-enhancing benefits. These might be mental, such as the ability to stay calm under pressure or focus for an entire race or match. Sometimes the benefits are physical ones – better balance, more efficient breathing or faster recovery times.

These benefits may be small, but sport is all about gleaning those extra few percentages that accumulate over time to boost overall performance or, as British Cycling's Performance Director Dave Brailsford famously put it: 'performance by the aggregation of marginal gains.'

In recent years an increasing number of professional cyclists have been adding yoga into their strength and conditioning routines. Bradley Wiggins practises yoga and Pilates moves to strengthen his core without adding muscle bulk, while Cadel Evans has credited yoga with forging his enviable flat back cycling stance.

Yoga for Cyclists is the first yoga manual for cyclists. Every stretch, pose, breathing method and concentration technique has been adapted for the sport. As a Yoga Sports Coach™ Lexie Williamson understands how to apply yoga to help cyclists achieve their own personal gains.

Cyclists are used to fine-tuning their bikes. By adding sport-specific yoga into the mix they now have the tools to fine-tune their bodies and minds to the requirements of the sport.

This book will be of benefit to both the professional and amateur cyclist. Coaches and physical therapists will also gain a greater insight into the use of yoga within modern day training methods. It is a great example of the increasing interest in yoga as 'prehab' for sportspeople and specialist performance training.

Hayley Winter,
Founder and Director of
Yoga Sports Science ® 2013

01

YOGA AND CYCLING

> *The best cyclists are very flexible. Fabian Cancellara is very supple. The longer your muscles, the more powerful you are and the fewer injuries you will get.*

Ryszard Kilpinski, Soigneur, Team RadioShack-Nissan,
Outdoor Fitness **magazine, November 2012**

This book is for cyclists looking for a strong, resilient but lean physique, supple enough to hunker down into a streamlined stance and ride in comfort for longer.

It is the first manual to adapt a range of yoga techniques specifically for cyclists, offering tailored stretches to release tight hamstrings, quads and glutes, alongside postures to bolster the core and create balanced whole-body strength.

Yoga for Cyclists also dedicates a chapter to easing out lower and upper back tension, and explores a range of endurance breathing techniques to maximise oxygen intake. In Chapter 10 ('Mental training') we learn how to forge a powerful, positive mindset, while the techniques in Chapter 11 ('Recovery yoga') recharge mind and body to return fresher and stronger.

Every technique is related back to cycling performance. Contributors include pro cyclists, as well as sports scientists, physiotherapists and sports psychologists, all working in cycling with teams and individual competitive riders.

So what can an ancient discipline like yoga offer the modern day cyclist besides an end to lower backache? Let's take a closer look.

A STRONGER CORE

A strong core is vital for cycling power, posture and injury prevention, particularly in your lower back region. Many cyclists have highly developed back muscles, and comparatively weaker abdominals. This muscular imbalance can create a range of lower back problems. A tired rider with poor core strength is also liable to slump in the saddle, placing undue pressure on shoulders and wrists. Many of the gymnastic-style exercises cyclists use to bolster the core, such as plank, locust or bridge, originate from yoga postures. These postures use just the body weight as resistance – no gym required. They have been selected to specifically strengthen core areas cyclists need to be resilient. These include the deep corset-like transversus abdominals, the lateral obliques (which create a stable, still torso), and the glutes and 'six-pack' rectus abdominals (which power hill climbs and sprints). Many of the core postures in this book have been designed to closely mimic the cycling stance in order to create sport-specific strength. See Chapter 8 for more on the cyclist's core.

Starting yoga 1: yoga kit

Yoga is very low maintenance when it comes to kit. If practising straight after a ride, just remove your shoes and socks and you are ready. Otherwise choose clothing that is stretchy and warm. But here are a few items that will be useful:

- a yoga mat
- a yoga belt, dressing gown cord or old tie
- yoga blocks or small cushions.

ABOVE: Cycling crunch

LEFT: Cycling plank

A FLATTER (AND HAPPIER) BACK

Cadel Evans, winner of the 2011 Tour de France, is well known for practising yoga to improve his form on the bike, especially to gain a 'flatter back'. But what exactly is a flat back, and how can you achieve one? According to Dr Chris Edmundson, a sports science lecturer and former competitive cyclist, it means avoiding an excessive 'lumbar kyphosis', or curvature of the lumbar (lower) back region. Picture a cyclist with a very rounded back craning his head to look ahead at the road. Not only does this posture create drag, but it is likely to cause pain in the lower back, upper back, shoulders and neck. Cyclists with a flat back are likely to have more supple back muscles, but also sufficient flexibility in their lower back, hips, glutes and hamstrings to perform an anterior pelvic tilt. Chapter 2 provides five yoga postures to facilitate a flatter back. This improved posture – as well as correct bike fit – will help alleviate lower backache, but there are also many yoga poses that increase comfort levels.

Your back is not designed to be held in flexion for prolonged periods, as it is in cycling; the supporting ligaments are stretched and weakened, placing stress on the intervertebral discs. This inevitably leads to tension, pain or more serious conditions, such as a slipped disc. Experiment with post-ride back tension releasers, such as drawing your legs in to your abdomen to massage your lower back. Or decompress the spine through lengthening full-body stretches – you can even hang from a doorframe. Then ease your back into extension by performing gentle backbends as this reverses the flexed position. Finally, introduce rotations and side-bends. Periodically moving the spine through its full range of motion, in combination with abdominal exercises, will vastly improve comfort levels on the bike. See Chapter 6 for more on back comfort, and see also Chapter 2 on tension-free cycling.

ABOVE: *Low back massage*

LEFT: *Cobra*

STRENGTH WITHOUT BULK

❝ Unlike straight sprinters like Chris Hoy, I need endurance over power, so I focus on avoiding bulking up. Even 1 kg of extra muscle can add expensive seconds to your time. In the gym you should focus on strengthening your core for 30 minutes each day, mixing up Pilates, yoga moves and using exercise balls. ❞

Bradley Wiggins, *The Sun*, 19 August 2012

Because yoga both strengthens and lengthens muscles, practitioners never bulk up or lose the range of motion around the joints. The result is long, lean muscles – a powerful yet pliable body, less susceptible to injury. Yoga postures also often strengthen multiple muscle groups at the same time, helping to correct muscle imbalances. This makes them a good choice for cyclists who have highly developed quads and backs, but weaker abdominals, inner quads or hamstrings.

In strengthening terms yoga postures can either be held statically or linked in a fast moving 'flow'. If you lack the patience for static stretching or strength work, this heart-pumping, sweatier style of yoga is the answer. Practise precision by studying the static postures in Chapter 7, then experimenting with a strength flow from Chapter 9. These are organised according to your goals, and include a 'sprint and climb' core sequence (see page 162) and 'cyclist's sun salutation' (see page 156) to promote cycling-specific flexibility and strength.

RIGHT: Side angle pose: strength and length

Starting yoga 2: how to breathe

You probably think you can do this already! While practising yoga, the correct way to breathe is slowly and through your nose. This helps engage the parasympathetic nervous system, which calms and focuses the mind. Many yoga classes will begin with some deep breathing to shift you out of a 'fight or flight' mode after a stressful day at work and into a more relaxed state, ready to start stretching and strengthening. In this mental state you are likely to be more body aware, and less likely to push or strain. This heightened awareness is an especially useful state of mind for athletes; it helps them to notice potential injury or muscular tightness before these niggles become an issue. When yoga teachers talk about 'a breath' they mean one inhalation and one exhalation. Teachers of dynamic or flowing yoga like ashtanga will ask you to synchronise the breath and movement (inhale in warrior 2 and transition into side angle pose on an exhale; see page 121. This is confusing to start with, but soon becomes automatic. Static stretching is simple: hold for between five and ten slow breaths, which equates to thirty to sixty seconds.

TENSION-FREE CYCLING

Tension in your shoulders, wrists, and upper and lower back drains precious energy and compromises pedalling efficiency and form. It creeps easily into these areas, especially on long, gruelling rides. Your body slumps, your arms can lock and your hands grip like a vice. This is an inefficient way to ride and can also strain your shoulders and neck. Rather than waiting to stretch after the ride, incorporate a range of small movements that will ease out this tightness as you ride. Alternatively, use the bike as a stretching prop to decompress your back or freshen up your legs for the next stage of the ride. In Chapter 2, physiotherapist Ian Brocklesby shows you some quick on-bike techniques to stay relaxed, while senior sports scientist Dr Chris Edmundson explores ideal cycling posture. Of course, muscular tension often stems from mental stress and this is where deeper breathing would help (see Chapter 3), or a little mental training (see Chapter 10). Only yoga addresses the athlete as a whole by linking the tightness in his shoulders to the thoughts in his head.

RIGHT: *2 x wrist stretches*

BELOW: *Extensor stretch*

FEWER INJURIES

Yoga is ideally 'prehab', as opposed to rehab. If you want to start yoga but have a specific injury or any pain, visit a physiotherapist or doctor first. If it's just a common problem like tight hamstrings, hips, quads or lower back then a regular yoga session will reduce your chances of suffering with the overuse injuries that plague cyclists, such as iliotibial band syndrome or piriformis syndrome. Yoga is especially beneficial if the postures are sequenced with cyclists in mind, focusing especially on these notorious tight spots. Because your legs are never fully straightened in cycling, your hamstrings get little chance to lengthen fully, meaning that they too are susceptible to tears and strains due to this gradual loss of elasticity. Knee problems are also common, mainly due to the imbalance of strength in your quads (Chapter 7 contains strengthening postures for the often weaker inner quads), although bike fit factors, such as incorrect saddle height, can also be to blame.

How to stretch

The most common questions on stretching are 'when?' and 'for how long?' However, correct technique is also important.

- **When?** The current thinking on 'when' is largely post-ride unless you have a specific area, such as the Achilles tendon, that would benefit from extra attention in the form of a pre-ride static stretch. Having said that, dynamic movements involving large muscle groups (such as sweeping the arms in a circle) are a great warm-up. A brisk marching action provides a similar benefit to your legs. In terms of maintaining flexibility, the muscles are warm and supple immediately after riding, so this is the optimal time to stretch. Don't wait until you've had a shower and got changed. If there is no floor space, stretch standing up, using the bike as a prop (see Off-Bike Stretches, page 32).

- **How long?** A cursory five seconds will make no difference, so hold for a minimum of thirty seconds to restore muscles back to their resting length. This equates to five or six slow breaths.

- **How?** Never bounce or jerk, as the muscles will contract tighter in response. Come into a stretch of mild discomfort or find the 'edge' of the stretch. If your face is contorted in pain you have gone too far – ease back. Don't fight it. Use props; for example, if your hamstrings are tight, lie on your back and loop a yoga belt or old tie around your foot. See leg and hip stretches (page 51) for more pointers on correct stretching technique. Finally, tune in to your breathing. Slow, deep breathing through your nose will further facilitate muscular release.

EFFICIENT BREATHING

Many people don't think about their breathing until it abruptly 'runs out', usually just before the apex of a hill. But by consciously controlling the rhythm and depth of the breathing you can transform it from an automatic function into a much-undervalued (and totally free) training tool. Many time trial cyclists synchronise the breath with pedal cadence to maintain a consistent pace (see Breath/Cadence Ratios, page 44). But all cyclists can learn how to breathe more efficiently. This basically means breathing slower and deeper to maximise oxygen intake. This can be done by breathing more using the diaphragm, but also creating a more supple torso that can expand into the back (see abdominal breathing, page 41, and back torso breathing, page 46). Dr George Dallam, a former USA Triathlon National Team

ABOVE: *Back torso breathing. Expanding the ribcage in an aerotuck position*

Coach and Professor of Exercise Sciences, argues that our basic instinct to pant rapidly is not the most economical way to breathe during running or cycling. Yoga has a host of techniques to make your breathing slower and deeper, some of which have been adapted in this book specifically for cyclists. See Chapter 3 for more on breathing.

FIT FOR LIFE, NOT JUST BIKE FIT

You love cycling. But can you kick a ball around without pulling a hamstring? Have your knees seized up when you stand up to leave the cinema? The fixed, linear nature of cycling can create a restricting tightness in your hips, back and shoulders. This lack of mobility can affect your ability to move freely when doing other sports and in life generally. This is especially the case if you have a desk-bound day job. Lots of sitting will make your hip flexors and hamstrings shorter, and place even more strain on your back. The human body is designed to move not just forwards but laterally (sideways). It should also easily extend (bend backwards) and rotate. With a joint's range of motion it's a case of stretch it or lose it, and while a curved back looks good on the bike, it's not so attractive as an everyday posture. Yoga moves the body systematically through all these planes to ensure that you are not just 'bike fit' but fit for life. Of course, any extra mobility gained through practising yoga will be beneficial for cycling too. A strong but supple cyclist can hold a correct, aerodynamic stance in more comfort, for longer. See Chapters 4–6 for stretches that will assist in achieving this.

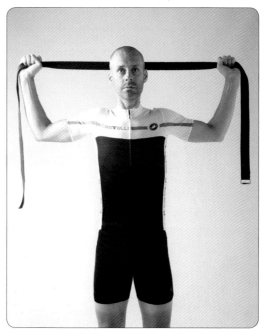

ABOVE: *Seated glute stretch*

RIGHT: *Pectoral stretch*

STRETCH, STRENGTHEN AND SWEAT

Stretching doesn't have to be dull. While it's a good idea to practise the postures in this book statically first, there are many forms of dynamic or faster-flowing yoga akin to the cardiovascular workout you love. Many athletes who feel cheated without a good sweat are drawn to styles of yoga such as ashtanga or power yoga, where postures are sequenced in a rapid flow. The increased pace and strenuous nature of these classes means precision can get lost. Cyclists may be particularly susceptible to overstraining their shoulders or lower back, if jumping between postures. A middle ground for those without the patience to hold static stretching might be to create your own flowing sequence of cycling-specific stretches and strength postures by linking a series of static ones – then practise it at a pace that suits you. Chapter 9 offers a few suggestions, including a cyclist's sun salutation to stretch your quads, hip flexors and back, while bolstering your core through cycling-specific movements. An added benefit of flowing between postures is that it trains the mind on the breathing – a skill that can be transferred onto the bike as a means to both improve breathing economy and focus.

BELOW: Cyclists sun salutation. A fast-moving squence to stretch and strengthen

TRAIN THE MIND

Some coaches argue that cycling success is as much as 50 per cent mental. That is to say, if two professionals are equally matched in terms of sheer hours of physical training, the cyclist with the toughest mindset is already the winner. We know that the mind often surrenders before the body is ready, and this nagging self-doubt ('it's too steep, I can't make it') is an issue for all athletes, but especially so in a gruelling endurance sport like cycling. Equally, the mind can be your best asset if it can be controlled and used to your advantage. Channelling and harnessing our random (and frequently negative) stream of thoughts is the underlying purpose of yoga. But creating a more focused mindset need not mean spending hours in the lotus position on a mountain top.

There are many mental techniques that can be practised even while cycling. Using visualisation, a rider can 'hook' the one in front with an imaginary fishing rod and reel him in. The commentary technique (page 172) sees a rider place himself as the star of a TV racing commentary – each move recorded in his head by a commentator ('nice and steady as he approaches the first bend'). All these techniques anchor the mind firmly to the action occurring at that very second. In a nutshell, this present-second awareness is the key to remaining positive, alert and aware on the bike. See Chapter 10 for more on mental training.

BELOW: Cycling success is up to 50 per cent mental

OPTIMISE RECOVERY

Professional cyclists, like all athletes, factor recovery time into their training schedule knowing that, after recharging their batteries, they return fresher and stronger. For cyclists also holding down a full-time job, or with families, finding time to switch off is not so easy; it's just not feasible to lounge on the sofa all day. Nor will you receive a daily massage from your own soigneur. However, there are many simple yoga techniques that will optimise the valuable recovery time you do possess, like stretches held for longer periods of time that require no effort. These 'restorative' stretches are perfect for both restoring muscle length and speeding up muscle recovery. They will also begin the process of winding down a busy mind for bed. A good eight hours' sleep is, after all, the best recovery tool, but if sleep proves elusive yoga has a wide choice of relaxation techniques, such as a 'tense and release' process, where muscle groups are first engaged so they can release deeper. Experiment to find the technique that best suits your personality. Good recovery is vital

ABOVE: *Wall inversion*

if you want to be strong and ready for the next day's riding. Knowing how to relax or meditate is also a useful skill for surviving life's general stresses. See Chapter 11 for more on recovery yoga.

BELOW: *Relaxation*

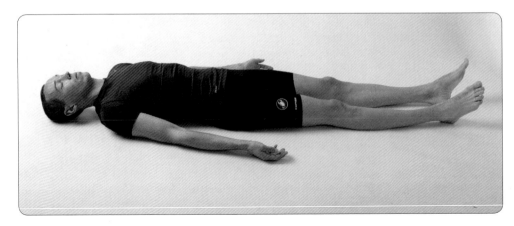

Starting yoga 3: the right class for cyclists

There are as many types of yoga as there are martial arts, so it's worth considering what you need from a class. If you are training intensively or have injuries, go for a gentle class with a focus on deep stretching like hatha yoga. To build strength and stretch look for dynamic styles like power yoga, vinyasa flow or ashtanga. Here's a guide to the main types and their relevance for cyclists.

- **Hot yoga** – Cyclists keen to shed pounds have been flocking to specially adapted studios heated to 105° Fahrenheit, with 35 per cent humidity. This sweltering heat aids deep stretching, but take care if you are overweight, drink a lot of water to stay hydrated, and don't overstretch. Search for 'bikram' or 'hot yoga' to find a local studio.
- **Ashtanga** – This style of yoga is strenuous, and follows the same pattern of postures or 'series', which becomes progressively more advanced as you gain experience. There's an emphasis on upper body strength, with lots of plank (see page 133) and dog (see page 70), so steer clear if your upper body is already tight from cycling; but athletes generally love the faster pace and competitive element of ashtanga.
- **Power yoga** – Suitable for 'type As', power yoga is the strongest, fastest style, and will build core, arm, back and leg strength. Similar to ashtanga, but the content may change from session to session. Again, be prepared to sweat (and possibly grunt and curse). Power yoga tends to be popular with men.
- **Vinyasa flow** – Like ashtanga and power yoga, vinyasa flow focuses on moving from posture to posture in flowing sequences, but is gentler. It's a good starting point for those worried they will find static yoga dull, but are not yet bendy or strong enough to brave the more strenuous styles.
- **Hatha yoga** – The gentlest style of yoga, 'hatha' will probably be a slower class with more static postures and an emphasis on the 'mental' side of yoga. A session will include breathing exercises, meditation or relaxation. Hatha is a great option if you are training hard and need to simply stretch and unwind.
- **Yoga for cyclists** – Obviously this is the ideal option if you can find a class for cyclists close by. If not, yoga for runners will offer many of the same benefits, although with less emphasis on releasing back, neck and shoulder tension. Yoga for cyclists should also focus on stretching your legs, especially your quads and hamstrings, and improving core strength. It may also touch on breathing or mental training.
- **Iyengar yoga** – A static style of yoga where postures are held for longer periods instead of one flowing dynamically into the next. This means more time on precision and alignment: great if you are injured. Holding postures builds strength too (isometrically), but this still form of yoga does require patience. Adrenaline junkies can find Iyengar slow compared with vinyasa flow, ashtanga and power yoga.

FLEXIBILITY CHECKS

Starting yoga 4: yoga verses Pilates

Cyclists are often told to improve flexibility or strengthen their core by doing yoga or Pilates, but are unclear on the differences between the two disciplines and which will benefit them the most.

If a stronger core is your priority, opt for Pilates, which was invented by Joseph Pilates in the early twentieth century. This is because a Pilates class focuses on exercises generated from the 'powerhouse' of abdominals, lower back and buttocks. That said, a Pilates class will include some stretching, and many of the core postures are also taught in yoga.

In you are injured and need precise, controlled exercises, Pilates is also a wiser choice as it centres on posture and alignment. Many yoga classes now feature fast-moving stretching and strengthening sequences, or flows, which means precision can get lost in the rush to keep up. However, if lack of flexibility is affecting your cycling performance – evident through poor cycling posture or tense, hunched shoulders – try yoga. A yoga teacher will spend a good proportion of the class lengthening tight leg muscles while teasing your back into backbends that reverse the hunched cycling stance. Being a wider mind-body discipline, you may also gain extra skills transferable to the bike, such as learning how to breathe more deeply and relax.

Flexibility check 1

This is a simple and quick way to discover where you are tight along the posterior chain of muscles, from the hamstrings up to the neck. Sit on the floor with your legs together and stretched out in front, toes pointing upwards. Relax your arms at your sides. Round your back and drop your head down so it hangs heavy.

Where do you most feel the stretch? Turn to the suggested chapter for targeted stretches.

1 The back of your neck (extensors) - chapter 5
2 Upper back and area around your shoulder blades – chapter 5
3 Lower back – chapter 6
4 Hamstrings – chapter 4

Flexibility check 2

To assess if cycling is causing your chest and shoulder muscles to tighten and shorten sit on the floor with your legs together and stretched out, feet relaxed. Take your arms behind you and rest your palms on the floor, fingers pointing to the back of the room. Find a comfortable width between your hands. Press your palms into the floor and lift your chest slightly. Draw back your shoulders. Look ahead.

Where do you most feel the stretch? Turn to the suggested chapter for targeted stretches.

1 'Pecs' or chest muscles – chapter 5
2 Shoulders – chapter 5
3 Wrists – chapter 5
4 Forearms – chapter 5

Flexibility check 3

To assess flexibility in the hips, hamstrings and quads, perform a basic runner's lunge position with the right foot in front and back knee resting on the floor (use a cushion to pad the knee if necessary). Place both hands on the front thigh and tuck your tailbone (sacrum) under. Sink your hips. Now sweep the left arm up and over into a side bend.

Where do you most feel the stretch? Turn to the suggested chapter for targeted stretches.

1 Hip flexors of your back leg (where your thigh joins your hip) – chapter 4
2 Outer hip of your back leg (glute medius/iliotibial band) – Chapter 4
3 Upper quads of your back leg (top thigh) – chapter 4
4 Hamstring of the front leg (under the front thigh) – chapter 4
5 Side of the torso – chapters 3 and 6

02

TENSION-FREE CYCLING

‘ People doing long rides don't know how to stop and stretch, and when to. They just keep grinding away even though they are slowing down and feeling miserable. You don't need a lot of flexibility to ride a bike, but it helps you feel a lot better. Stretching can bring you back a bit, when you are feeling slow. ’

Bob Anderson, Stretching Inc, quoted in
Zinn's Cycling Primer, **Lennard Zinn (Velopress)**

This chapter offers practical techniques to stay relaxed as you ride, by tackling the energy-sapping tension that can creep into your shoulders or wrists after hours in the saddle.

Techniques range from a coasting hamstring stretch to subtle postural adjustments to keep your lower back happy for a few more miles. These 'on-bike' techniques are not designed to fully restore the length of muscles tightened by hours on the bike. That remains the job of the static post-ride stretches featured in the lower body, upper body and recovery chapters of this book. However, what they will provide is comfort if the wrists are aching or your neck is sore, and a great opportunity to freshen up tired legs for the next stage of the ride.

Because cycling tension is so closely linked to bike fit and posture, we will also explore the subject of ideal cycling stance, with a little help from the experts.

STAYING RELAXED WHILE YOU RIDE

Tension in your shoulders, back, arms or legs wastes energy and compromises efficiency. Stay as relaxed as possible while you ride by making the following small adjustments, suggested by UK-based physiotherapist Ian Brocklesby, who works with the Rapha Condor Sharp cycling team.

EYES

Prevent headaches and sore eyes by wearing sunglasses in summer and clear glasses in winter. This stops squinting caused by glare and harsh weather and keeps the facial muscles relaxed.

NECK

Keeping your eyes on the road, sit up and place the fingers of one hand on your chin. Tuck in your chin, applying a little pressure through your fingers, to reduce tension in your neck and stretch ligaments. Hold for five seconds and repeat five times.

SHOULDERS

Roll and shrug your shoulders to relieve tension in the trapezius and levetor scapulae muscles. Drawing your shoulder blades together will open your chest and aid breathing. Open up your chest like this periodically to prevent diaphragm compression and loss of oxygen intake.

ARMS

Bent arms give a degree of shock absorbency and comfort by not transferring every bump in the road onto your shoulder girdle and neck. Let the arms and shoulders relax while coasting. Avoid a vice-like grip on the bars while standing in hill climbs. This tenses the whole upper body and wastes energy. A bent elbow arm position, especially if they are drawn slightly in to the sides of your torso, also aids diaphragmatic movement. Shake out the arms regularly.

HANDS

Alter your hand position frequently. Cycling for prolonged periods with your hands resting on either the hoods or drops can lead to neck extension. This can cause numbness and tingling in your hands, and fatigue and strain in your neck and shoulders. To alleviate this, sit up on the bike and, keeping your eyes on the road, rotate your head from side to side, and up and down. Avoid the power grip as this can cause eventual damage to your wrists and hands.

QUADS

Efficiency and cadence are the keys to leg comfort. Regularly shift the gears to maintain a steady 70–90 revolutions per minute (rpm) as this faster cadence is less likely to strain your knees and is energy efficient. Pushing big gears, especially on hills, puts tremendous strain through the patella-femoral (kneecap) joint.

GLUTEALS

Clench and relax the glutes or buttocks while coasting to take the tension out of these muscles after prolonged cycling.

ANKLES

Unclip one foot at a time and rotate them in circles to loosen off your ankles.

RIGHT: Alter your hand position frequently

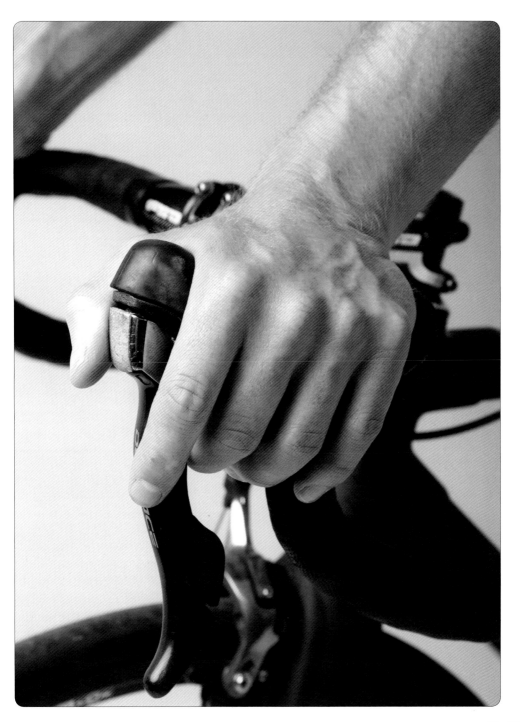

IDEAL CYCLING POSTURE

According to Dr Chris Edmundson, former competitive cyclist and senior sports science lecturer at the University of Central Lancashire (UK), finding a cyclist's optimum riding posture is a complicated process, 'part art and part science'.

Edmundson, who collaborates with British Cycling, explores a range of factors during an average assessment of two and a half hours with a cyclist, including his measurements, injuries and bike fit.

Flexibility is also an important component. 'In order to achieve a comfortable and efficient cycling posture adequate flexibility in your hamstrings, gluteals and lumbar spine are essential', explains Edmundson. 'The ability to achieve relatively free motion deep hip flexion and an anterior pelvic tilt and are also important.'

But even if a rider is supple, poor riding position may be due to incorrect bike set-up. According to Edmundson, some cyclists deliberately set the handlebars low in a bid to reduce drag. 'There is often an excessive focus on becoming aerodynamic', he explains. 'But due to lack of flexibility in the posterior chain the natural curves of the spine are lost and lower back discomfort is often experienced.'

One major key to improving cycling posture and gaining the ideal flatter back, according to Edmundson, is to focus on 'reach'. Due to lack of flexibility, cyclists often set their bicycle with a reach that is too short. This results in kyphosis, or curvature of the lumbar (lower) and thoracic (mid) spine. This back shape forces the cyclist to over extend the head to look up, causing pain in the neck and shoulders.

By extending their reach (determined by saddle setback, top tube length, stem length

Poor posture – hunched shoulders and a rounded back

Improved posture – relaxed shoulders and a flatter back

and handlebar length), cyclists with limited flexibility can achieve the desired anterior pelvic tilt and avoid an excessively rounded back.

The final ingredients for optimum cycling posture are lumbar strength and supple hamstrings, as Edmundson explains: 'This elongated position requires well-developed back muscles to stabilise the pelvis and vertebral column, and adequate hamstring length to prevent posterior rotation of the pelvis.'

Five yoga poses for a flatter back

Cyclists often talk about the ideal 'flat back' posture, which essentially means avoiding an excessive 'lumbar kyphosis', or curvature of the spine in the lumbar (lower) region. This overly rounded or hunched posture is more likely to cause lower back pain and make it harder to breathe properly. These five yoga postures will increase flexibility in your lower back, glutes and hamstrings to facilitate a flatter back posture. Lumbar strength – built up here through the locust pose – is also required in order to hold this ideal posture in place. Bolster it further with targeted abdominal strengtheners from Chapter 8.

1 Runner's lunge – to stretch your hip flexors

Start on all fours. Step your right foot up in between your hands and, keeping your fingertips in contact with the floor, sink into the lunge. For a deeper variation, lift your upper body, take your hands to your hips or front thigh and tuck your pelvis under. Hold for five breaths.

2 Pelvic tilt – to increase lumbar flexibility

Lie on your back with your legs bent and arms by the sides. On an inhalation keep your pelvis on the floor but raise your abdomen off, so there is a gap under the lumbar, or lower, spine. On an exhalation press your abdomen into the floor so the lumbar spine flattens. Perform four times, synchronising the movement with the breath.

3 Strap hamstring stretch – to lengthen the hamstrings

Loop a strap around the sole of your left foot. Bend your right leg. Straighten your left leg as much as your hamstring allows. Walk your hands up the strap until the arms are straight. Hold for five to ten breaths.

4 Figure four stretch – to stretch the glutes

Move onto your back. Place the feet on the floor, hip-distance apart. Lift the right leg and lay the right ankle on the left thigh. Flex the right foot. To deepen the stretch interlace the fingers behind the back of the left leg and draw both legs towards the abdomen. Hold for five breaths.

5 Locust – to build lumbar strength

Lie face down with the arms by the sides, palms face down. On an inhalation raise your upper body and legs off the floor but remain looking downwards. Hold for five breaths. Repeat four times.

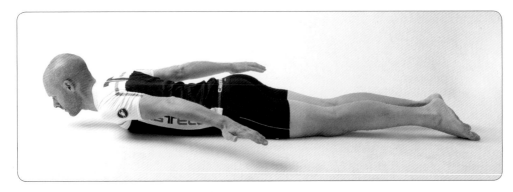

MID-RIDE STRETCHING

Stretching is usually postponed until after a ride, but if your lower back aches or your quads are screaming halfway through a cycle, why wait?

These quick stretches will allow you to keep riding, maintain range of motion and improve comfort levels. Try standing up in the saddle while you are coasting and drop one heel down to alleviate that dull ache in the calves. Or pause at the traffic lights to perform some slow shoulder rolls. Alternatively, wait until you stop to refuel and use the bike as a prop to perform some off-bike stretches.

On-bike stretches

Perform the on-bike stretches in a flat, traffic-free section of road for as long as you feel stable and safe.

LOWER BODY

▶ **Hamstrings:** Rise out of the saddle, straighten your legs and move your hands down to the drops, turning the body into a right angle. Keep your feet level on the pedals and lean in until you feel your hamstrings pulling in the front leg.

▲ **Calf:** From the hamstring stretch position bend the front leg and straighten your back leg, dropping your heel towards the floor until you feel a stretch in the calf.

▲ **Backbend:** To tackle tightness in the back while still in the saddle, draw your shoulders back, arch your back a little, drawing your shoulder blades down, and lift your hips. This mimics a mini yoga 'cat stretch' movement, temporarily countering the strain caused by maintaining a flexed spinal position for hours on the bike.

UPPER BODY

You probably perform your own instinctive upper body movements to relieve your shoulders, upper back or neck muscles. But, if not, here are a few suggestions. Some are easily performed while riding, but save others for a traffic light stop, when you can take both hands off the handlebars and stretch without compromising balance.

Shoulders: Keeping your hands resting lightly on the hoods and the arms slightly bent, perform some slow shoulder rolls by moving your shoulders in a circle. Or shrug your shoulders by lifting them up under the ears and squeezing before releasing down.

Neck: Tilt your head a little from side to side to stretch the sides of your neck. Or keep your eyes on the road but tuck your chin slightly in to stretch your back of your neck. Hold for a few seconds, then release.

Chest: At traffic lights, pause to sit up in the saddle. Take both hands behind you and interlace your fingers. Draw your shoulders back to really 'open' your chest and stretch your pectoralis muscles, which become short and tight during cycling.

Off-bike stretches

Your bike is the perfect stretching partner. The top tube is the right height to ease tightness out of your upper back, shoulders, quads and glutes and the muscles will be warm and receptive to stretching. Perform off-bike stretches on a rest break to ease out muscular tightness from your shoulders and back and put the freshness back into your legs. Either lean your bike against a tree or wall or, if no support is available, brace the bike by placing one hand on the handlebars and one on the saddle.

▼ **Quads:** Lean the bike against a wall or tree or hold it still with one hand. Place your right hand on the saddle and bend your left leg. Hold onto your left foot with your left hand, tuck your tailbone under and level your knees. Remain here, pushing your hips forwards. To go deeper push your foot into your hand to pull it back as if drawing back a bow.

▲ **Hip flexors:** Grip the bike with both hands, taking them shoulder-width apart. Step your left foot back as you bend your right leg, as if performing a lunge. Remain here pushing your hips forwards until you feel a stretch at the top of your back thigh. Switch sides.

▲ **Glutes:** Bend your left leg as if performing a high one-legged squat. Lift your right leg off the floor, turn your knee out and lay your right ankle on top of your left thigh. Flex your left foot to protect your knee joint. For a more intense glute stretch, sit lower, but be mindful of knee pain.

▶ **Back:** To ease tension from the back and shoulder muscles that maintain cycling posture, keep your hands on the top bar and walk backwards until the body drops into a right-angle position. Tuck your tailbone under and draw your hips away from the bike. Experiment with arm width: move your hands closer for a deeper shoulder stretch. Sway your hips slowly one way, then the other to target the side of your torso and deep shoulder muscles.

03

ENDURANCE BREATHING

' *Since starting yoga my breathing has seen a dramatic improvement when pushing hard on the bike. Up until now I would take myself to the very limit and my breathing would very much show that, being loud and forced. Using different techniques I have learnt to control the flow of breath in both directions and feel more in control when in the red.* '

Phil Sykes, time trial specialist, UK

Breathing is unlikely to crop up in a conversation about cycling training techniques. After all, isn't inhaling and exhaling completely automatic? Most cyclists rarely think about their breath apart from when it abruptly 'runs out' in a sprint or hill climb.

But next time you ride, take time to tune in: your breathing is supplying continuous feedback regarding factors such as cardiovascular fitness and pace. It tells you when you are overexerting and equally when you are slacking and could pick up speed.

The breath is also an undervalued performance tool. Cyclists can consciously control their breathing, transforming it from an automatic function into a valuable asset by experimenting with the exercises in this chapter.

BREATHING FOR ENDURANCE

These 'breath training' techniques are adapted from traditional yogic breathing, or pranayama exercises, and have various functions:

- to act like a metronome to maintain pace and rhythm
- to distract the mind from exhaustion on long rides
- to maintain mental focus, especially during racing
- to prevent muscular tension creeping into your shoulders and arms, keeping you efficient and relaxed on the bike
- to increase your breathing volume, rather than rate.

All these techniques share this last common goal of creating a slower, deeper breathing pattern. Inhaling and exhaling deeper – as opposed to faster – is contrary to our instinct to take quick gulps of air when the going gets tough, but it is a much more efficient way to breathe.

ABOVE: *Athletes pant to reduce the urgency to breathe.*

BREATHE DEEPER, NOT FASTER

According to Dr George Dallam, a former USA Triathlon National Team Coach and Professor of Exercise Science at Colarado University, cyclists 'pant' because they want to reduce their sensation of breathlessness. They are reducing their blood CO_2 levels, but believe (falsely) that they are also upping their oxygen intake.

'Athletes pant to reduce the urgency to breathe', explains Dallam. 'However, rapid, shallow breathing also reduces the transfer of oxygen into the blood because oxygen diffuses more slowly. Shallow breathing leaves too little time for full diffusion and reduces the number of capillaries available as well.'

In her book *Breathe Strong, Perform Better*, physiology professor Alison McConnell explains that elite cyclists are able to increase breathing volume rather than rate:

❛ A characteristic of professional cyclists is that the shift towards higher breathing frequencies does not occur and they are able to meet increased demand for breathing by increasing their breath volume. The maintenance of breath volume may reflect a higher training status of the cyclist's inspiratory muscles, and this may be a key factor in minimising the energetic cost associated with breathing, thereby enhancing performance. ❜

The term 'inspiratory' refers to the diaphragm and intercostal muscles between the ribs used during inhaling, although some muscles in your neck are also involved (see box on the diaphragm, page 40).

SUSTAINING PACE

Cycling is an endurance sport, with 'endurance' classified as 'the capacity to sustain effort over a long period of time'. Elite cyclists – both in time trials and the flat section of a road race – frequently use their breathing to maintain a rate of around 90 rpm by synchronising pedal cadence and breath (see breath/cadence ratios, page 44).

They use their breath to maintain speed and momentum, and play with various breath-to-pedal ratios, according to the terrain. For them,

breath training is another way of gaining the edge over competitors or training partners. It might be a marginal one, but a gain is a gain.

STAYING CALM AND FOCUSED

A final benefit of deeper breathing is that it calms the nerves by triggering the parasympathetic nervous system rather than the opposing 'flight or flight' survival response triggered by short, fast shallow breathing (and adrenaline).

Adrenaline may well be coursing through your veins while dodging shopping traffic on a Saturday morning. This danger element is part of the sport's attraction. But a brain in fight or flight mode doesn't make wise, quick decisions. A cyclist in a state of constant high alert will also burn out faster than his fellow teammates.

LEFT: Deeper breathing helps you to stay calm and focused.

OFF-BIKE BREATH TRAINING

Transforming the breath from an automatic function to a performance tool to be used strategically during cycling takes time and patience.

Before embarking on 'on-bike' techniques, work through the following 'off-bike' steps to first create a more supple torso that facilitates deeper breathing, and then practise breathing slower and deeper.

Breathing properly is a subtle business, best practised away from the distractions of the road, but persevere; it is well worth dedicating a few minutes of your training schedule to your most undervalued asset: your lungs.

Technique 1: stretching your torso

A degree of flexibility in the muscles and connective tissue wrapped around your torso is necessary for increasing the depth of breathing as it allows your ribcage to expand and contract freely. Cyclists are not known for their supple back muscles (or indeed their love of stretching), but extremely tight muscles around your back and torso will prevent your lungs from inhaling fully by constricting your ribcage. These three simple stretches will ease out tightness in these areas as well as the sides of your torso, which rarely get a good stretch. Aside from creating a supple torso, they feel great after a long ride.

Side: Sit on the floor with your legs crossed. Slide your right arm out to the side. Inhale and sweep your left arm up and over as you come into a side-bend. Stay for five (or more) slow breaths, trying not to tip forwards or back. Repeat on the other side.

Front: Roll shoulders back and interlace your hands behind your back (or hold on to a tie or dressing-gown belt) to stretch your chest muscles. Lift your chest and raise your chin a little without tipping your head back. Take five breaths.

Back: Interlace your fingers in front, palms facing you. Tuck your chin in to stretch the back of your neck and really round your back so you can feel your shoulder blades spreading apart. Take five breaths.

Technique 2: how do you breathe?

The most energy-efficient way to breathe is roughly 80 per cent with your diaphragm, the primary respiratory muscle. The secondary respiratory muscles in your neck and upper chest, like the sternocleidomastoid and trapezius, should take up the remaining 20 per cent of the task.

This 80/20 ratio is one to aim for while riding, but breathing like this will also keep you cool and calm in the face of life's general stresses. Notice that when you are faced with a stressful situation or emergency the breathing feels higher in your chest. When we are anxious, the ratio is more likely to be 50/50, accompanied by raised shoulders, a tightness between your shoulder blades, and even around your neck and jaw.

These same physical responses happen on the bike: your shoulders become tense and rise up, the arms lock and your hands adopt a white-knuckle grip on the handlebars. It's an energy-sapping, inefficient way to breathe that creates unnecessary tension.

TYPES OF BREATHING

Upper chest: Someone breathing primarily using the secondary respiratory muscles tends to take short, shallow breaths and might feel tension in the neck, shoulders, between the shoulder blades and even around the jaw.

Chest breathing: We are taught that taking a deep breath means inflating your chest, but chest breathing isn't the most natural or efficient way to breathe and is likely to trigger the body's 'fight or flight' stress response.

Abdominal breathing: Natural, efficient and relaxing; breathe more from the abdominal region and you are shifting more of the breathing role to your primary respiratory muscles: the diaphragm and abdominal muscles.

WHERE DO YOU BREATHE?

Lie down with your legs bent and feet on the floor, hip-distance apart. Simply place one palm on your abdomen and one palm on your chest. Close your eyes. Notice which hand moves as you breathe. Most people will notice movement in both the abdomen and chest, but one may predominate. Ideally you are working towards a completely still upper hand, with your lower hand visibly rising and falling on each inhalation and exhalation.

The diaphragm: made for endurance

The diaphragm, a large dome-shaped muscle that sits in your chest like a parachute, comprises 80 per cent slow-twitch fibres, making it ideal for endurance sports. Slow twitch fibres are more efficient at using oxygen to liberate energy over a long period of time. It requires a lot less energy to breathe primarily using the diaphragm than the delicate respiratory muscles around your neck, upper back and upper chest that we tend to recruit when shallow breathing or panting. This is because these secondary muscles contain more fast-twitch fibres, which fire quickly but tire easily. These muscles are also less efficient at bringing about changes in lung volume, meaning that they must work relatively harder than the diaphragm to generate a given breath volume. In more upright cycling positions diaphragmatic or 'belly' breathing is beneficial, just as it is in running (see abdominal breathing while on the bike, page 43).

However, if you drop lower into a more aerodynamic stance, with your belly compressed and working to stabilise the core, abdominal breathing becomes more challenging. One method of continuing to breathe deeper and lower is to inhale more into the side and back of your torso (see technique 3 in on-bike training on page 47).

RIGHT: *Abdominal breathing becomes more challenging when you drop lower.*

Technique 3: abdominal breathing

Aim: This simple technique shifts your breathing more into the abdominal region and thereby increases the role of your diaphragm. Once mastered, experiment with 'belly breathing' on the bike.

Lie down with your legs bent and feet on the floor, hip-distance apart. Place both palms on your abdomen so that your fingertips touch. Close your eyes. As you breathe in, allow your belly to rise so your fingertips move slightly apart. As you breathe out, let your belly deflate and your fingertips reconnect. Breathe only through your nose. Repeat five times.

Technique 4: optimising lung capacity

Aim: We can't make our lungs bigger but we can optimise our existing capacity. The average resting person uses just ten to fifteen per cent of their lungs to breathe. This exercise focuses on taking a more complete inhalation.

STEP 1

Lie down with your legs bent and feet on the floor, hip-distance apart. Repeat the abdominal breathing technique with your palms on your belly, taking four breaths.

STEP 2

Then move your hands to the side of your ribcage. Press lightly so you can feel your ribs. Focus on inhaling into your palms. Notice how your ribcage expands both outwards and sideways into your hands as you breathe in. Take four breaths.

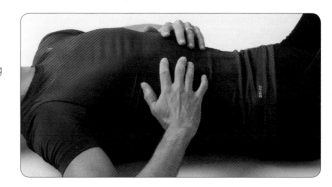

STEP 3

Finally, place your fingertips on your collar bones and imagine you can breathe into this upper section of your chest. Take four breaths. Now link all three techniques by inhaling first into your abdomen, then 'rolling' this inward breath into your lower, then your upper chest. Slowly release the exhalation through your nose and begin again.

Technique 5: exhaling longer

A simple trick to practise at home while doing deep breathing exercises such as abdominal breathing, and later transfer to the bike through breath/cadence ratios, is to exhale longer. Why?

Exhaling longer:

- Expels more CO_2.
- Triggers a deeper inhalation, thereby kick-starting a deeper, slower breathing pattern.
- Aids recovery when you abruptly run out of breath during a hill climb or sprint, and literally feel there's no air left in your lungs.
- Helps avoid the instinct to pant rapidly through the mouth – an inefficient method of transferring oxygen to the muscles.
- Calms your mind, keeping your thinking clear and focused.

Sit or lie down with your legs bent and feet hip-distance apart. Take a deep abdominal breath or roll the inhalation from abdomen to your upper chest (see technique 4: on page 41). Now purse the lips as if preparing to breathe out through a small straw and release the exhalation in a slow, controlled manner. Continue breathing out until you feel your lungs empty. Notice how much slower and deeper the next inward breath is. Repeat five times. Resume normal breathing, but take a second to observe the relaxing effect.

ON-BIKE BREATH TRAINING

The next step is to take breath training onto the bike, but do continue to practise the off-bike breathing techniques. Experiment to find the right on-bike exercise for you, and for more breathing techniques that also train the mind, go to Chapter 10.

Technique 1: on-bike abdominal breathing

Abdominal breathing focuses on using the diaphragm as the body's primary breathing apparatus. The principle is simple: as you inhale allow your abdomen to expand. As you exhale draw in. Practise abdominal breathing off the bike first, as described in technique 3 on page 41. Then use it while concentrating on other activities, such as driving or working at a desk so that it becomes automatic by the time you are ready to try it on the bike. Abdominal breathing while cycling works best in a more upright stance when your abdomen is not compressed. Also, take your hands a few centimetres wider on the handlebars to allow more space for your lungs. Upright abdominal breathing is a useful recovery technique, say, after a sprint, when you need a few rapid lungfuls of air. As you breathe out and draw your belly in you are also helping to stabilise the core.

Technique 2: breath/cadence ratios

Many cyclists intuitively link pedal revolutions with an internal rhythm such as a song stuck on rewind that plays over and over in their heads. This is a useful way of maintaining momentum, but not as technical or reliable as tapping in to your breathing. During a time trial or flat stage of a road race, elite cyclists often synchronise breathing rhythm and pedal cadence to maintain speed and momentum.

This breath/pedal cadence technique uses a counting system (ratio) that encourages a slightly longer exhalation on flat terrain. This can be switched to an equal inhale and exhale for hill climbs, when oxygen demand rises sharply.

As well as maintaining speed on the flat, linking the breath and cadence concentrates the mind on hill climbs/long training sessions distracting you from negative thoughts and burning thighs.

Exhaling a little longer also expels more CO_2 and forces a deeper inhale, thereby slowing the breathing generally.

Fix your attention on your right foot. Each cadence is one count. If the terrain is flat, start by inhaling for a count of two, linking each count with the turn of your foot. Then exhale for a count of three with the following three turns. Try to sustain this tempo. Want to go deeper? Inhale for a count of three and exhale for a count of four.

It's important not to force the body into a ratio it is not ready for. If you feel any discomfort or dizziness performing the breath/cadence ratio technique then it's probably too long. Shorten it, and then gradually work your way back up.

For hill work you will need an equal and shorter ratio such as inhaling for a count of two and exhaling for a count of two. Experiment: your ratio will depend on dozens of factors such as lung capacity, cardiovascular fitness, gears, counting speed and terrain.

You can assist this process of lengthening your exhalation by controlling the flow of air out of your mouth. Rather than having your mouth wide open, narrow the air passage by slightly pursing your lips as if blowing through a straw.

To go a step further, use the same process for your inhalation, sucking the air in through your 'straw'. It's a halfway house between gulping air through the mouth and nasal breathing. Introduce this very gradually over a period of time and on select, gentle, flat phases of a ride, when warming up or cooling down.

According to Alison McConnell, another reason to link the breath and pedal cadence is increased power. She explains that cyclists can time the exhalation to coincide with a pedal down stroke especially when climbing. As you breathe out, the abdomen engages, and you use this extra core stability to create more power as you push down. It's the same principle used by rowers, who exhale as they draw the oars through the water.

Of course, sometimes an exhale will coincide with the upstroke, so the jury is out as to the exact physiological benefits of linking breath and cadence. There have been few scientific studies on the subject, but McConnell concludes: 'The entrainment of breathing to pedal cadence occurs more often and for longer periods in experienced cyclists, suggesting that it may provide some advantage.'

RIGHT: *Linking the breath and pedal cadence can increase power*

Technique 3: back torso breathing

Shallow breathing, where the cyclist has his mouth open and is panting in a bid to suck in as much oxygen as possible, is partly down to the rider's posture. With your chest and abdomen partly compressed by a rounded spine and shoulders it is harder for you to breathe deeper than runners with their upright stance.

The classic hunched position adopted when cyclists use aerobars makes deep breathing even more challenging. The abdominal organs compress your diaphragm, restricting its movement, so there is less room for your abdomen to expand. The abdominal muscles are also engaged, stabilising the core, making it hard to use your diaphragm to 'belly breathe'.

These factors can combine to produce fast but shallow, upper body breathing or panting. Aside from not supplying adequate oxygen to the muscles, breathing using the delicate secondary respiratory muscles uses precious energy.

The aim of this technique is to create alternative space for your inhalation by breathing more into the side and back of your torso. It comprises four stages, from torso stretching to bike. Don't skimp on the stretching phase as cyclists are notoriously tight in this area, and locked back muscles won't budge when you want them to expand with the breath.

Back breathing is more subtle than abdominal or chest breathing, but persevere: performed properly it will allow you to stay hunkered down for longer without having to come up for air, and will create upper body stillness.

1   **Torso stretches:** As described at the beginning of this chapter (page 38). Stretch the front, side and back of your torso.

2   **Resistance band breathing:** For this technique use a rubber resistance band tied tightly around your lower ribs or place your palms on the ribs, spreading your fingers so that you can really feel your ribcage. You can find resistance bands, such as Thera-Band, in sports shops or online physiotherapy and Pilates equipment stores. The resistance band should be wide and flat to the body, and tied quite tightly around your lower ribs. Close your eyes and slowly breathe in, expanding your ribcage outwards either into the band or your palms. As you exhale, feel the band resistance slacking or the pressure move away from your hands. Take five breaths. Notice if your movement increases on each effort.

3 **Back breathing, all fours:** Replicate the aero position on all fours, with your forearms on the floor. Interlace your fingers or separate your hands so your forearms are parallel as they would be on the bike. Repeat step 2, either with or without the band, but focus this time on expanding the back ribs on each inhale. Alternatively, ask someone to place their palms firmly on your lower ribs and concentrate on inhaling into them. Don't expect large movements, especially at first. Take five breaths, aiming for a few millimetres of increased movement on each breath.

4 **Back breathing, turbo trainer:** Repeat step 3, but this time on the turbo trainer or gym bike either with or without the resistance band. Try back breathing without pedalling initially, but once you are really feeling increased thoracic movement as you breathe begin to incorporate it into your training. The next step would be to combine this technique with the breath/cadence ratio technique so that you can further control your breathing rate.

5 **Back breathing, road:** When you've practised enough away from the distractions of cars, weather and other riders, take the technique onto the road. Work now to further slow and deepen the breath by controlling the flow of air in and out of the mouth. Purse the lips slightly and blow the exhalation out slowly. This will help extend your exhalation and work with your back breathing to keep your torso still and steady.

Investigation: cycling and nasal breathing

The use of nasal breathing in sport remains a controversial subject among running and cycling coaches. There are large phases of a bike ride that necessitate the mouth to be open to take in as much oxygen as possible, especially during sprinting or hill climbing. But could nasal breathing be used during gentler phases of cycling, such as the warm-up or cool-down stage?

In his book *Body, Mind and Sport*, John Douillard argues the case for nasal breathing during exercise. He claims that the fast mouth breathing or panting does provide an abundance of oxygen to your middle and upper lungs, but the accompanying accelerated heart rate means there is less time for your lungs to perform a gaseous exchange. This makes rapid mouth breathing an inefficient way to breathe during endurance sports.

Dr George Dallam has experimented with nasal breathing in his own training for years, completing sprint triathlons (750 m swim/20 km bike ride/5 k run) breathing entirely nasally. Dallam claims never to suffer coughing fits after training or racing and rarely gets ill due to the natural filtering design of your nose which traps and removes viruses and other pollutants. He is relaxed during races and, most importantly, says his performance has improved:

' For practitioners of hatha yoga breathing through the nose is not a new concept. As a sport scientist I came to learn that there is value in trying to use slower, deeper abdominal breaths – and then fairly recently determined through my own experience that this pattern of breathing can be created 'automatically' as a consequence of using nasal breathing. '

Dr George Dallam, former USA Triathlon National Team Coach and Professor of Exercise Science at Colarado University

THE QUESTION IS, HOW IS NASAL BREATHING ACCOMPLISHED?

It's the transition that's the tricky bit. The body may take up to a year to fully adapt, and in the meantime it can feel like you are desperately trying to suck air through two tiny straws (although wearing a nasal strip can help). In cycling, nasal breathing is further restricted by your nose running when riding in cold, frosty weather.

Nasal breathing feels initially unnatural because slower and deeper nasal breathing elevates carbon dioxide levels in the blood. This creates an urgency to breathe, or 'minor anxiety', as Dallam puts it. However, according to Dallam, our carbon dioxide receptors adjust to this in time and this sense of urgency disappears.

Still interested? Introduce nasal breathing very gradually; it may take up to a year for the body to fully adapt. First breathe nasally while performing the 'off-bike' deep breathing exercises in this chapter. Then slowly introduce nasal breathing to light intensity, non-cycling activities like taking the dog for a brisk walk.

The next step is to introduce it into cycling at the very beginning of a warm-up, or in the last few seconds of a cool-down. Increase this time in increments and stop if there is any dizziness or discomfort. Then experiment with small periods of nasal breathing on flat stretches of road. Finally, treat it as a strategic tool: breathe nasally at low intensity to reserve energy, but open the mouth to gulp air when you need a quick fix of oxygen to tackle a hill, accelerate or sprint. For one to one guidance on incorporating nasal breathing into training seek the advice of a Yoga Sports Coach™ (to search the global network of coaches go to www.yogasportscience.com).

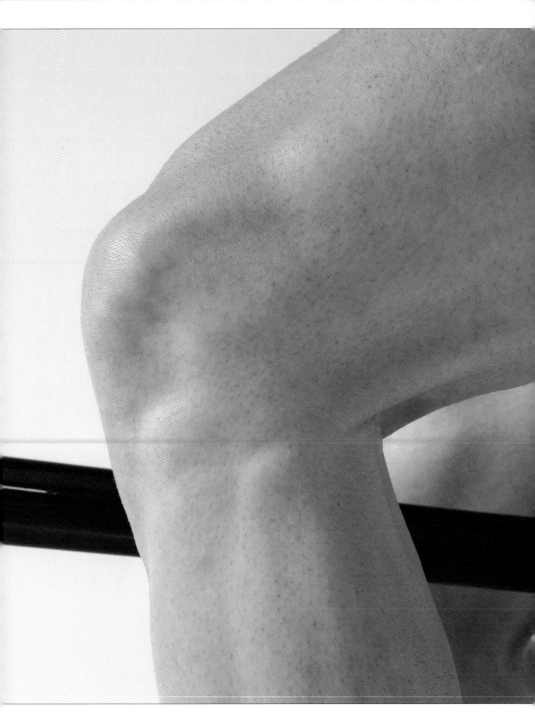

LEG AND HIP STRETCHES

' I have a large repertoire of stretches so I can pick and choose. It also depends where I am; do I have a wall, chair or couch? What tools are available? Rollers or tennis balls? My stretching kit is small and compact to guarantee its place in my travel bag. I often stretch for 45–60 minutes a night to calm down and increase blood flow to my fatigued muscles. A consistent stretching routine allows one to tap into early warning signs and avoid long-term imbalances that may spark into acute pain down the road, often at the height of the season! '

Benjamin Chaddock, Team Exergy, USA

The four 'quads' are the cyclist's hardest-working muscles, as is evident from the bulging thighs of pro riders. This is because your quads kick-start the pedal cycle. The glutes and calves take over as the pedal approaches six o'clock. Then your hamstrings sweep the pedal back to nine o'clock. Finally, your hip flexors lift the pedal back to the top for another cycle.

THE QUADS

As they are the cyclist's prime pedalling muscle group, it's worth devoting a little time and energy looking after the rectus femoris, vastus lateralis, vastus medialis and vastus intermedialis. Gentle post-ride stretching will increase blood flow to your quads, helping to repair micro tears, and restore the muscles to their resting length.

However, compared with a simple hamstring stretch, lengthening your quads can feel awkward. This is partly because they pass through your knee joint, so some stretches place pressure on your knees. That's fine if the joint is supple and injury-free, but it can exacerbate any existing problems. The golden rule is if there's any discomfort, exit the stretch and substitute one with less knee impact.

The quad section of this chapter contains a range of stretches that should be accessible to all cyclists. As with hamstring stretching, the recipe for successful stretching is to *hold for 30 seconds or a good five to six slow breaths*. Like all stretching, a little patience reaps rewards.

You will need: a strap (cotton yoga strap or old tie) and a foam block, or cushion. Remove socks and shoes.

Quad stretches

BASIC QUAD STRETCH

Loop the strap over your right shoulder, ready for use. Stand with your feet hip-distance apart, facing a wall. Rest your left fingertips on the wall. Bend your right leg and reach back for your foot with your right hand. If it's too far away, loop the strap around your foot. Level your knees and tuck your pelvis under.

SHOULDER/QUAD STRETCH

Set up the stretch as before but move a little further away from the wall. Bend your right leg and reach back for your foot with your right hand, using the strap if necessary. Walk your left fingertips up the wall and lean into the wall until you feel a stretch in your shoulder and upper arm. Keep your pelvis tucked under. Walk your fingertips back down to rise up.

CYCLIST'S QUAD STRETCH

This is a great all-rounder for cyclists as it takes the compressed cycling posture and reverses it by opening up the entire front of the body, including your chest, shoulders, hip flexors and quads. Tuck your chin down to release tension in your neck and you are stretching every area prone to tightness on the bike. The final element is the balance. This does take practice, but persevere as the simple act of standing on one leg strengthens your feet and ankles, and hones balance skills. If you are wobbling, turn side-on to the wall and just a few inches away for support.

Move away from the wall. Lift, spread and lay down your toes of your right foot to widen your balancing base. Gaze at a fixed point and bend your right leg. Now either loop a strap around your foot or reach back and grip it with your right hand. Tuck your tailbone under and level your knees. Slowly reach round with your left hand so both hands are now holding your back foot. Draw your shoulders back to open your chest. Tuck your chin slightly downwards. Breathe slowly and steadily. Exit gradually and – if you are still balancing – hug your right leg into your abdomen for a second before releasing your foot to the floor.

LYING QUAD STRETCH

Stretching while lying on the side is often the most comfortable position for those with tight quads. Have the strap nearby and lie on one side. Balance by scissoring your legs rather than stacking one above the other, bend your top leg and hold your foot, or loop the strap around it. Extend your lower arm and rest your head on it.

The kneeling series

The simple act of kneeling provides your quads with a gentle stretch, making it a good general sitting position for cyclists. But it does place pressure on your knee joint and ligaments, so those with knee injuries, or very stiff quads, may find it uncomfortable or impossible. If this is you, just practise step 1, with plenty of padding, or opt for standing quad stretches. As the series proceeds, the postures become stronger, so continue to monitor your knees.

You will need: a strap and some foam yoga blocks or cushions.

STEP 1: KNEELING

Sit in a straightforward kneeling position with your heels together. To lessen your knee flexion, place one or more cushions between your buttocks and heels. Or separate your heels and lay two to three yoga blocks horizontally between your lower legs. Rest your palms on your thighs and sit tall. Gaze ahead or close your eyes.

STEP 2: HALF KNEELING QUAD STRETCH

From kneeling, release your right foot out and place it on the floor so your leg is still bent. Take your hands behind you, fingers pointing backwards. Lift your hips off the floor to stretch your left quad. Look down or ahead. Hold, lifting your hips and chest on every inhalation.

STEP 3: FULL KNEELING QUAD STRETCH

Remain kneeling and take your hands behind you, fingers pointing backwards. Lift both hips off the floor, tucking your tailbone under. Look down or ahead. Slowly lower down. This pose can also be done dynamically by lifting on an inhalation and lowering on an exhalation.

STEP 4: HALF RECLINING QUAD STRETCH

Extend your right leg down along the floor, keeping your left leg in a kneeling position. Sit tall and monitor any discomfort in your left knee. If your knee is happy, tuck your tailbone under and lower slowly back to rest on the forearms. Exit slowly, pressing onto both hands to rise up evenly.

STEP 5: QUAD AND HAMSTRING STRETCH

For a time-saving stretch, straighten just your left leg. Exhale and fold into a forward-bend until you feel your hamstrings stretching or loop a strap around the sole of your left foot. Keep your back straight and take your chest – not your nose – towards your knee. Rise up slowly.

THE HIP FLEXORS

Many cyclists don't stretch their hip flexors, but the psoas and iliacus at the top of your thighs help lift your leg on every pedal stroke. Short, tight hip flexors can pull your pelvis out of alignment, leading to potential back problems. A runner's lunge is the answer, and provides the added benefits of an 'ease-in' gentle quad stretch and a backbend to release tension in the lumbar area. You may need to pad your back knee by placing a cushion or block under it. For a stronger version that ticks more boxes try the lunging backbend (see page 118).

RUNNER'S LUNGE 1

Start on all fours. Step your right foot up between your hands and, keeping your fingertips in contact with the floor, sink into the lunge by dropping your hips.

RUNNER'S LUNGE 2

To deepen the stretch lift your upper body and take your hands to your hips. As you hold, continue to tuck your tailbone under and lean slightly backwards.

RUNNER'S LUNGE 3

Return your upper body to an upright position. Place your right hand on your right leg and sweep your left arm over. Hold, tucking your pelvis under.

RUNNER'S LUNGE 4

Drop your fingertips back down to the floor and lift your back knee. As you hold, focusing on sinking your hips towards the floor.

THE HAMSTRINGS

Hamstring injuries are common in cyclists and are frustratingly slow to heal, so stretching is crucial to maintain length and elasticity for injury prevention. Unfortunately, hamstrings can also be frustratingly slow to release: a cursory five-second pull on semimembranosus, semitendinosus and biceps femoris won't make any difference, so *stay in the stretch for a good thirty seconds, or five to ten slow breaths.*

Standing hamstring stretches

90° HAMSTRING STRETCH

For tight hamstrings, and any lower back issues, try this half-forward-bend. It can also be performed facing a wall with your hands resting on the surface. Stand with your feet hip-distance apart, toes facing front. Inhale, and on an exhalation slide your hands down your thighs to rest just below your knees. Tuck your tailbone in to minimise the lumbar curve. Look downwards. Bend your knees, engage your abdomen and raise yourself up to standing like a weightlifter.

FULL FORWARD-BEND

To stretch deeper repeat the 90° stretch, but slide your hands down until your fingertips touch the floor either side of your feet, bending your knees as much as you need to. Alternatively stack several blocks next to each foot and rest the fingertips on this raised surface. Release your head. To exit first engage your abdomen, and bend your knees further then rise back up to 90°. Pause here, then raise all the way up to standing with a flat back.

HALF PYRAMID

Half pyramid is a deep hamstring stretch that also strengthens your back. Begin with your feet hip-width and step your right foot forward. Keep your toes (both feet) facing front. Sweep the arms behind your back and hold onto your elbows. On an exhalation forward-bend to a 90° position. Take six slow breaths, or more if well-balanced. Maintain a long, straight spine. To exit engage your abdomen, bend the front knee and rise up.

FULL PYRAMID

Repeat half pyramid, but release your fingertips all the way down to the floor, placing them either side of your feet. If they don't reach the floor, bend the front leg more or place a block – or stack of books – under each hand. Release your head.

CHAIR PYRAMID

To decompress the spine repeat half pyramid but rest your hands on the back of a chair. This takes the balance element out of the posture so you can focus solely on your hamstring and back/shoulder stretch – very satisfying after a long ride. A wall, tree or kitchen worktop can substitute for the chair.

How to stretch tight hamstrings

1 **Bend your knees:** If performing a forward-bending hamstring stretch, always bend your knees to take the strain off your lower back.

2 **Sit on a block:** Perch on the edge of a block or cushion in the seated stretches. This helps tip your pelvis forward into an alterior tilt, which, again, takes the pressure off your lower back.

3 **Use a strap:** In seated and lying hamstring stretches go for comfort, and a more targeted hamstring stretch, by looping a yoga strap, old tie or dressing-gown belt around the sole of your foot.

4 **Don't round your back:** In seated forward-bends imagine folding your chest (not your nose) to your knee. Rounding your back in the hope of inching your nose closer to your knee just strains your lower back.

5 **Don't bounce:** In response to every bounce, your hamstrings will contract tighter. Instead be still and breathe slowly to facilitate a slow, gradual release.

6 **Have patience:** It takes thirty seconds for your hamstrings to release. Use this time to close your eyes, tune into the breath, and recharge mental and physical batteries.

Floor hamstring stretches

SEATED HAMSTRING STRETCH

Sit on the edge of a block or cushion and loop a strap around the soles of your feet. Straighten your legs, or have a small bend in your knees. Sit tall and inhale. As you breathe out, inch your hands down the strap until you feel your back wants to round and your hamstrings are pulling. Stop. Relax your head, close your eyes and hold, subtly moving your chest – not your nose – towards your knees. If you find any discomfort in your lower back, then rise up higher.

SEATED HAMSTRING/ HIP STRETCH

Remain in the same position but bend your right leg and take the sole of your foot to the inside of your left thigh. Place a cushion or block under your knee if it is hovering off the floor. Sit tall and inhale. As you breathe out walk your hands down the strap until you feel your back rounding and your hamstrings are pulling. Relax your head, close your eyes and breathe slowly, encouraging your chest gradually closer to your knee. Rise up.

STRAP HAMSTRING STRETCH

This is a simple and relaxing way to stretch your hamstrings. Loop a strap around the sole of your foot, as much as the hamstrings allow. Bend the other leg and place the foot on the floor (a), or extend it along the floor with the toes pointing upwards (b). Walk your hands up the strap until the arms straighten. Hold for five to ten slow breaths.

a

b

THE ILIOTIBIAL BAND

If you've been cycling for a while you may have encountered the iliotibial band (ITB). This tight strap of connective tissue runs from your hip, through the outside of your knee and attaches to your shin. It slides over a bony projection on every pedal stroke, and is easily inflamed. If you ride for two hours at a cadence of 90 rpm, the ITB will cross your knee *21,600 times*. Iliotibial band syndrome, or ITBS, is called 'runner's knee', but it is just as much a cyclist's issue. ITBS manifests as a pain around the outside of your knee. A physiotherapist may recommend both strengthening and stretching exercises as well as foam rolling (see Chapter 11). As a preventative measure, however, stretch the ITB regularly while lengthening your hip flexors, quads and hamstrings, as tightness here increases the risk of ITBS. This fibrous band is a little elusive, but here are two exercises that should locate it and stretch it.

STANDING ITB STRETCH

Stand with your feet hip-distance apart and side-on to a wall. Step the outside foot across so your legs are crossed at your thighs. As you inhale, sweep your outer arm up. On an exhalation, side-bend towards the wall so that your fingertips rest on its surface. Remain here breathing slowly.

RUNNER'S LUNGE 3

This side-bending lunge is a useful time-saving stretch for cyclists as it lengthens both the IT band, the outer hip muscles and the hip flexors – all common tight spots.

From an all fours position step your right foot up between your hands and raise your upper body. Tuck your tailbone under. Breathe in and sweep your left arm up. As you exhale tip to the right and hold.

If the pose is uncomfortable with your knee resting on the floor, perform a higher lunge from standing by simply stepping your right foot forward, bending your knee and sweeping your left arm over.

Other ITB poses include Figure Four Stretch, described in the glutes section (following page) and Pigeon (page 66).

The iliotibial band and saddle height

ITB pain can be caused by a factor as simple as incorrect saddle height – another good reason to invest in a bike fit session. According to Dr Chris Edmundson, sports scientist and performance advisor to Rapha Condor Sharp, this fibrous strap of connective tissue can be aggravated if the saddle is set too high. You may also risk posterior knee pain and biceps femoris (a hamstring) tendonitis over time from this saddle setting. Position the saddle too low, however, and you risk anterior knee pain, patellofemoral pain, quadriceps tendonitis and an overstretched Achilles tendon.

THE GLUTES

The gluteus maximus, the largest of the three buttock muscles, provides downwards power in the pedal cycle. The other glutes – medius and minimus – rotate and move your leg out sideways, but on the bike they control unwanted movement to keep your legs pumping in a smooth forwards motion.

Figure four stretch

Lie on your back with your legs bent and your feet on the floor. Lift your right leg off the floor, turn your right knee out and lay your right ankle on top of your left thigh. If this feels tight, shuffle your left foot forwards. Engage or flex your right foot, as this will protect your knee joint and focus the stretching work on your hip. Maintain flexion in your right foot and ease out if there is any discomfort or pain. To go deeper proceed into the next stages, closely observing your knee.

- **Stage 1:** Maintain pose for five slow breaths.

- **Stage 2:** Take your right hand to your right knee. Keep your foot flexed and apply a little pressure to deepen the stretch.

- **Stage 3:** Hold behind your left thigh, lift your left foot off the floor and draw both legs in towards you.

- **Stage 4:** Transfer your hands in front of your left shin, but only if you can comfortably lay your head back down.

SITTING AND STANDING VERSIONS

Stretch the glutes at the office or while watching TV by performing the figure of four exercise seated. Sit upright on the edge of the seat. Bend your right leg, turn your knee out and lay your right ankle on top of your left thigh. Keep your foot flexed to protect your knee joint. To lessen the stretch, shuffle your left foot away. To deepen the stretch, maintain a straight spine and lean over your legs. A standing version can also be performed using the bike as a prop (see Chapter 2).

PIRIFORMIS

Cycling and piriformis syndrome

The piriformis is located within the glutes and deserves a special mention as it can cause problems for cyclists. Piriformis syndrome, where the muscle irritates the sciatic nerve that passes through it, causing pain or numbness in your buttocks and down the outside of your leg, is a common complaint. Causes include sitting for long periods on a hard surface (like your saddle), improper bike fit, poor cycling posture, weak hip muscles and lack of stretching. If you have pain that originates in your buttocks and spreads down the back of your leg then see a physiotherapist or doctor. He may recommend a rest from cycling, stretching or massage.

Locating the piriformis

Finding the piriformis in order to stretch can be tricky. If you have good hip mobility the easiest way is to lie on your back and cross your thighs (just as you would crossing your legs sitting on a chair). Then draw both legs into your abdomen. You are looking for a stretch right in the middle of your buttocks. Still don't feel it? If your right thigh is crossed over your left, rock an inch to your left. Rock the opposite way with your left thigh crossed over. If it's impossible to cross your legs, perform figure four stretch and rock to the side in a similar way.

Alternatively, try pigeon pose. This yoga posture is fantastic for cyclists as it ticks so many muscle boxes, including your hip flexors, glutes, iliotibial band and adductors or inner thighs. However, it does require healthy, supple knee joints, so approach it cautiously, moving through the following steps and sticking with one step if your knees or hips say 'enough'.

Five steps to pigeon pose

STEP 1: FIGURE FOUR STRETCH

Lie on your back with the legs bent and feet hip-width. Lift the right leg and lay the right foot on top of the left thigh. Flex the right foot. Stay for five breaths. Deepen the stretch by interlacing the hands behind the left thigh and drawing both legs into the abdomen and take a further five breaths.

STEP 2: RUNNER'S LUNGE

Move onto all fours, step your right foot up between your hands and sink your hips. Relax your back foot.

STEP 3: RUNNER'S LUNGE HIP STRETCH

From runner's lunge move your right foot out to your right. Place your right hand inside your foot and sink your hips down deeper to feel a strong stretch in your hips and groin. To go deeper, lower onto your forearms with the arms parallel or fingers interlocked.

STEP 4: GENTLE PIGEON

Revert to runner's lunge and slowly lower your right knee to the floor. Then slide your right foot slightly out to the left, making sure that your foot is flexed to protect your knee joint. Bend the arms a little, but stay high and watch for any discomfort or pain in your knee joint.

STEP 5: PIGEON

If your knee is comfortable and you want to go deeper, lower onto your forearms with the arms parallel or fingers interlocked. Or stack one hand on top of the other and rest your forehead on the back of your hand. Try to relax into the posture. Ease slowly out.

THE ADDUCTORS

The adductors, or inner thigh muscles, may not feature in many stretching repertoires, but can become surprisingly tight while cycling and running due to their leg-stabilising role.

LOW SQUAT

If you have no knee problems, a low squat provides both a deep hip and adductor stretch, and lengthens the calf muscles making it a useful time-saver. Stand with your feet wider than hip distance, toes turned out. Bend your knees and gradually sink into a low squat. Then rest your fingertips on the floor in front for balance.

COBBLERS POSE

Sit tall, with a block or cushion under your hips if your back rounds. Bring the soles of your feet together. The closer your heels to your pelvis, the stronger the pose, so if it feels too tight, move your feet further away. Interlace your fingers around your feet (or grasp higher up around the ankles) and lengthen the spine by lifting from the crown of your head. Hold without pressing or bouncing your knees.

LOWER LEG STRETCHES

Calf stretches

The two calf muscles – gastrocnemius and soleus – apply a downward force on every pedal stroke, which explains why they are so clearly defined in elite cyclists. If you suddenly increase the intensity or length of a ride and forget to stretch you'll soon feel that tightness in the calves. This puts the calf muscles at risk of injury, as well as the Achilles tendon into which they insert. Like hamstrings, calves take time to lengthen, and need regular and diligent stretching. The solution is variety: pause on steps and drop one heel down; on a rest stop grip the bike and perform a high lunge by stepping one foot back and pressing your heel into the ground (see page 33). Alternatively stretch the calves, hamstrings and improve upper body strength with the downward dog calf sequence (see over the page).

CALF SQUAT

A straightforward way to stretch the calves – provided there are no knee issues – is to stand with your feet together and then bend your knees and lower into a squat. Rest your fingertips on the floor for balance, drawing your heels towards the floor.

ROLLED MAT STRETCH

Move to the middle of your yoga mat or towel and, starting at the front, roll up half of it. Keep your heels on the mat, but place the ball of your foot on the roll. This may be enough of a calf stretch. If you want to go deeper, and lengthen your hamstrings, slide your hands down to your knees so the body forms a 90° angle. Bend your knees and slowly rise up.

Calf stretching with downward dog

Downward-facing dog is a well-known yoga pose that is ideal for stretching the calves. It also works your upper back, shoulders and arms. However, downward dog can feel a lot like a plank (see page 133) for cyclists. This is due to the fact that if the hamstrings and back are stiff the body weight shifts more onto the shoulders and hands (the last thing you want after a big ride). Pick a gentler calf stretch if dog feels too intense in the upper body or 'walk the dog' (see below) by bending one leg and drawing the other heel down.

1 DOWNWARDS DOG

Begin on all fours. Turn your toes under, spread your fingers wide and lift your hips up towards the ceiling so your body forms a V shape.

Draw both heels down to the floor. If dog feels like a plank, with too much weight on your shoulders, bend your knees a little and try to shift your weight onto the back of the body.

2 WALKING DOG

Perform downwards dog as above but bend your left leg and press your right heel to the floor. Switch sides, bending your right leg and pressing your left heel down.

Then move faster from heel to heel, stretching alternate calves. Walking Dog is a good option if the hamstrings or calves are very tight. It can also be used as a pre-ride warm up.

THE SHINS

The anterior lower leg muscles help lift the pedal during the 'recovery' phase of pedalling. However, if you have a knee injury or kneeling is uncomfortable/impossible, try the standing version.

STANDING SHIN STRETCH

Place your hands on your hips. Step your left foot in front and bend your knee. Come onto the front of your back foot and push your ankle into the floor, as if you were dragging your foot behind you.

KNEELING SHIN STRETCH

Sit on your heels with your knees together. Place your hands on the floor behind you, fingertips facing either forwards or to the back of the room. Lift your knees until you feel a stretch in your shin area, and anterior ankle and foot muscles. Maintain pose for as long as is comfortable.

UPPER BODY STRETCHES

' We massage the whole body – not just the quads and calves, but also the back and arms. People think cycling is only done with your legs, but the tension goes through your whole body. '

Ryszard Kilpinski, Soigneur, Team RadioShack,

***Outdoor Fitness* magazine, November 2012**

Picture a road cyclist side-on and it's clear to see why your upper back, shoulders and neck can ache after hours in the saddle. The cycling stance requires us to hold our heads in extension to gaze ahead while the delicate wrist muscles help support what can be half the weight of your upper body. Time trial cyclists take this stance to extremes by tucking into a lower, more aerodynamic position, leading to increased neck and upper back tension.

Therefore, while the hard-working leg muscles undoubtedly deserve our attention when it comes to stretching, it's important not to neglect your upper body. Incorporate some of the techniques in this chapter to prevent imbalances in your neck and shoulders, which cause riding discomfort, overuse injuries and imperceptible postural changes such as rounded shoulders. This chapter offers a variety of at-home stretching techniques, including a series using a strap or old tie, and a doorframe sequence to bring your upper body back into balance.

Ensuring that your bike set-up is correct will also keep tension out of your upper body. Ask a bike fit specialist if your handlebars are set too low compared with the seat height. This is a common cause of wrist pain, as is having the seat pointed too far downwards, which places pressure on the wrists and forearms. See Chapter 2 for pointers on posture and bike fit.

THE NECK

I've never forgotten hearing a story about a team cyclist whose neck extensors were so weakened by craning to look ahead at the road he was forced to fix a strap from the rear of his helmet to his upper back just to hold his head up.

It's an extreme case and, thankfully, neck stretching is simple, can be done anywhere (including the office desk) and provides relief to tight muscles. The stretches in this section focus on the extensor and rotator muscles responsible for lifting and turning your head.

Neck stretch sequence

SLOW MOTION ROLLS

Drop your head down so that your chin tucks in and, in slow motion, roll your head in a semi-circle around to your right shoulder. Lower your right ear to your right shoulder, and pause here for five breaths. Repeat, working your way around to your left shoulder. Never tip your head back. Repeat frequently: on the train, at the desk and on the bike at traffic lights. Try closing your eyes and imagining each individual neck muscle stretching in turn. With neck stretching, the slower, the better.

LATERAL STRETCH

After performing a few slow motion rolls, pause with your head tilted to your left side. Sweep your left arm up and place your palm gently onto your head to ease it deeper into the side stretch. Stay for five breaths. Deepen the stretch by lowering your left shoulder, and play with straightening your left arm and moving it a little behind you. Repeat on your right side.

DIAGONAL STRETCH

Remaining upright, turn your head slightly to your left. Sweep your left arm up and across the back of your head on a diagonal angle. Place your palm at the back of your head and draw your head down diagonally. Stay for five breaths. Rise up and repeat on your right side.

EXTENSOR STRETCH

A fantastic stretch for cyclists as it reverses the extended head position. Maintain an upright spine and drop your head slowly down until your chin tucks in. Remain here breathing steadily, and go no further if this is deep enough. To advance, sweep both arms up and interlace your hands behind your head. Relax your arms so their extra weight increases the stretch.

ROLLING DOWN

Remain with your palms behind your head and begin to let your spine move down in slow motion until you feel the stretch spreading to your upper back. Pause and keep breathing steadily. Then take your time to uncurl back up into your upright start position and release your arms.

ROTATIONS

Finally lift your head so you are gazing straight ahead. Inhale, and as you exhale, turn your head to look over one shoulder, keeping your chin level. Stay for five breaths and repeat on the other side.

SHOULDERS

Your shoulders bolster your upper body as you cycle, not only holding it still while your legs pedal, but also contributing to the climbing effort as you sit up and pull on the handlebars. Aside from releasing tension, it's important that a cyclist's upper back and shoulders are not only supple but also strong, especially if holding the aero tuck position – see the aero tuck sequence from Chapter 8 (page 142) to make this vulnerable area more resilient.

Like the neck stretches and shoulder rolls, most of these shoulder techniques – like shoulder rolls – can be done anywhere and are good general warm-ups for cycling, so perform them whenever you remember. For the shoulder strap series you will need a yoga strap (a simple strap made of cotton), an old tie or a dressing gown belt.

Post-ride tension releasers

SHOULDER ROLLS

First break the rolling action down into sections. Move your shoulders forwards, tucking your chin in and allowing your upper back to round a little. Next lift your shoulders right up under your ears and squeeze. Finally, draw them back and slide them back, and slide your shoulder blades down your back. Now move faster in fluid circles. Repeat five times. Vary by placing your palms on your shoulders.

ARM SWEEPS

Take your arms by the sides and, keeping them straight, sweep them forwards and up on an inhalation, and back and down behind you on an exhalation in a circular motion. To release tension, breathe through your nose as you sweep up and blow the exhale slowly out of the mouth on the downwards movement.

ARMS WIDE

Take your arms out to the sides, shoulder-height and spread your fingers wide. Come into a gentle standing backbend by engaging your legs, tucking your tailbone under and leaning slightly back. Work on moving your hands further back, out of your line of vision. Keep the breath flowing smoothly throughout.

SHOULDER WRAP

Inhale and take your arms wide as before. As you exhale cross your right arm over your left and wrap your arms tightly in a hug. Tuck your chin in and round your back. Stay for five breaths. Release and take your arms wide. Repeat, but cross your left arm over right.

Moving deeper

'EAGLE' ARMS

This yoga pose advances the shoulder wrap and may not be feasible if your chest or biceps are well developed. If manageable, eagle is like giving yourself a deep back/shoulder massage. It targets not only your shoulders, but also your neck extensors and the hard-to-reach rhomboids around your shoulder blades.

As before, inhale and take your arms wide. As you exhale, cross your right arm over your left, but higher up. Instead of giving yourself a hug, aim for contact between your palms. Remain looking ahead. Stay for five (or more) breaths. Repeat by crossing your right arm over your left, or experiment with the variations below:

- **Variation 1:** On an inhalation, lift both arms directly up, and then on an exhalation lower back to the start position. Repeat four times. Switch sides.

- **Variation 2:** Breathing steadily 'windscreen wipe' the eagle arms from side to side. Repeat four times. Switch sides.

- **Variation 3:** Perform a twist by moving your eagle arms to your left and turning your head to your right. Switch sides.

- **Variation 4:** Return to the start position. Tuck your chin in and round your back. Switch sides.

- **Exit gradually** by unwrapping your arms in slow motion. Counter pose by sweeping your arms wide and performing some shoulder rolls.

SHOULDER RELEASE

Another gem for cyclists. Stand with your feet hip-distance apart and interlace your fingers behind your back. Inhale and lift your chest. Exhale, bend your knees and come into a forward-bend while raising your arms. Relax your head and stay for five or more breaths. If your hamstrings are tight, bend your knees further and rest your abdomen on your thighs to concentrate on your shoulder stretch. To exit, drop your hands to your lower back, draw your abdomen in and rise up with a straight back. If this is uncomfortable or you can't lift your hands off your back, try the stretch using a strap (see the strap series opposite).

SHOULDER HANG

To release general upper back tension stand with your feet hip-distance apart, bend your knees and come slowly into a forward-bend. Keeping your knees bent, relax your head, fold your arms and sway slowly from side to side like a pendulum. Let your arms be heavy. To exit, release your arms so that they dangle freely, draw in your abdomen and uncurl up to standing, raising the head up last.

CROSSOVER STRETCH

This stretch requires a good degree of hamstring flexibility! From standing, tip into a forward bend, keeping the knees slightly bent. Move the arms behind the knees and cross them at the wrists. Now slide both hands through the legs and grasp the shins. Let the head hang. Round the back for a more intense back and neck stretch. Exit slowly, bending the knees deeper, engaging the abdomen before uncurling to standing. Raise the head up last.

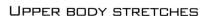

The strap series

It's much easier to access upper body stretches with a strap, especially if you are stiff or muscular around your chest and shoulders. Don't own a cotton yoga strap? Alternatives include a physio-type rubber resistance band, an old tie or a dressing gown belt. This sequence not only works your shoulders, but also lengthens the anterior shoulder and chest muscles, which can become short and tight in cycling.

Stand with your feet hip-distance apart and hold the strap with your hands a good shoulder-width (wider if your shoulders are tight) apart, palms face down.

STEP 1

Inhale and sweep your arms up until the strap is roughly overhead. Exhale and return your arms. Repeat four times.

STEP 2

Inhale and sweep your arms up. Exhale and drop your right arm towards the floor so you are side-bending to your right. Inhale back to the centre and repeat on the other side.

STEP 3

Inhale and sweep your arms up overhead, as in step 1. Exhale and bend your arms into right angles. Remain here breathing steadily and work on drawing your elbows gradually backwards, just out of your line of vision. Ensure your pelvis stays tucked under. Gaze ahead. Slowly release and perform some shoulder rolls.

STEP 4

From Step 3, bend the right arm so that the right hand drops behind your head. Work your left hand up your back in between your shoulder blades and grip the strap higher up. You may be able to let go of the strap and interlock the hands, but take it gently as this is a deep shoulder and triceps stretch. Unravel your arms slowly and repeat on the other side.

STEP 5

End this sequence with a more accessible version of the shoulder release stretch. Take the strap behind you, hands shoulder-width apart, with your palms facing forwards. Inhale, and on an exhalation bend your knees deeply and tip into a forward-bend while raising your arms. To exit, drop your hands to your lower back, draw your abdomen in and rise up with a straight back.

End the series by performing some slow shoulder rolls.

DOORFRAME STRETCHES

This series of stretches really targets your chest, especially pectoralis minor and major. These muscles can become shortened in cycling due to the flexed shape of your torso, and stretching them can feel intense. You will also feel a lengthening effect in the anterior shoulder muscles.

CHEST/SHOULDER STRETCH 1

Stand tall in the middle of the doorway, feet hip-width apart. Straighten your arms and extend them out at shoulder-height, placing your palms on the wall surface either side of the doorframe. Inhale, and as you exhale lean the whole body forward through the doorway, keeping your arms straight. Ensure your abdomen is slightly engaged and your tailbone is tucked in. Stay for five to ten slow breaths.

CHEST/SHOULDER STRETCH 2

Repeat as before, but position your arms in a higher 'V' position.

CHEST/SHOULDER STRETCH 3

Move slightly to the left of the doorway, raise your left arm up and bend it into a 90° angle. Place your palm on the doorframe and rotate the body away. Repeat on your right side.

THE WRISTS AND ARMS

Carpal tunnel syndrome and ulnar neuropathy ('handlebar palsy') are common overuse injuries in cycling due to the constant pressure placed on the wrists. If you are experiencing any pain, numbness or tingling in your hand, forearm and fingers, then a sports physiotherapist should be the first step. These wrist stretches – like all stretches – are best used primarily as a measure to prevent overuse injuries. In preventative terms, keeping the wrist in neutral or straight and changing hand position every fifteen minutes while you are cycling will also help. Other measures include cultivating a strong core to support the wrists, and even wearing padded gloves.

Wrist stretches

These stretches will stretch both the muscles underneath the forearm that flex or bend the wrist and those on the upper side of your forearm that extend or lift your hand.

WRIST FLEXOR (STANDING)

Stand tall with your feet hip-distance apart. Straighten your right arm in front at shoulder height. Extend your hand with your fingers pointing upwards. Now use your left hand to hold your fingers and draw them back towards you. Switch hands.

WRIST EXTENSOR (STANDING)

Repeat as before, but this time point your right fingers down. With your left hand hold your fingers and bend your hand further. Switch hands.

WRIST FLEXOR (KNEELING)

Start from a kneeling position for a more intense wrist flexor stretch. Prepare to place your palms on the floor in front with your fingers pointing back to your knees. Start by placing just your fingertips on the floor and very gently proceed to lay more and more of your palm onto the floor, if this is comfortable. When you hit a good stretch hold, then slowly peel your palms off the floor.

WRIST EXTENSOR (KNEELING)

Remain kneeling but perform the stretch palm face upwards so that you gradually lay the back of your hand onto the floor. Hold, then slowly peel your hands off the floor.

PRAYER FLEXOR STRETCH

Remain kneeling and place your palms together at chest height in a prayer position. Press your palms together and slowly lower your hands until your elbows form a 90° angle.

EXTENSOR/FLEXOR COMBINATION

Interlace your fingers, palms face down and chest-height. Pull your hands slightly apart as if your fingers were stuck together with glue and you can feel some traction. Then, maintaining this traction, alternately flex and extend (bend and draw back) the wrists.

WRIST ROLLS

Make fists with your hands and slowly rotate them to ease tension from the wrists. I also find wrist rolls release tension after holding the plank position (see page 134).

TOTAL UPPER BODY STRETCH

I'd like to end this chapter with a fantastic four-in-one posture for time-pressed cyclists. This deep shoulder-opener will also stretch the wrist flexors and pecs, and release back tension. Be warned: the second version is intense (it is based on a posture called 'the rack'), so don't try it if you have a shoulder injury.

STEP 1

Sit with your legs outstretched, feet engaged and toes pointing up. Sweep your arms behind you, fingers pointing to the back of the room. The closer you take your hands, the deeper your chest/shoulder stretch. Press your hands into the floor and lift your chest slightly. Draw your shoulder blades closer. Remain looking ahead, or tuck in your chin slightly to stretch the back of your neck. Stay for five to ten slow breaths. Exit the pose slowly, ease down onto the floor and hug your legs into your abdomen to stretch your lower back.

STEP 2

Repeat step 1, but this time walk your hands further back to increase the intensity in your shoulders. When you find a deep (but comfortable) stretch, stop and lift your chest. Draw your shoulder blades closer. Look ahead or keep your chin tucked in. Stay for five breaths. Repeat a third time, walking the hands further away, or exit then slowly ease back and roll your shoulders and wrists.

BACK COMFORT AND FORM

> ❝ People who know me may remember all those yoga exercises I do. No one understood why I spent so much time putting myself into those strange positions. Well, it's to improve my form on the bike. I sit on the bike with a much flatter back now than I used to three or four years ago, for example. ❞
>
> Cadel Evans, BMC Racing Team US,
> and Tour de France winner 2011, *Ride Cycling Review*

Yoga is fantastic for preventing cycling-related backache and, practised regularly, will vastly improve comfort levels on the bike, as well as helping to create better form (see Chapter 2 for more on the 'flatter back').

The road cycling stance is an aerodynamic dream, but this streamlined body shape is demanding on your back. Holding the spine in flexion for hours at a time can take its toll. For cyclists this usually manifests itself as a dull ache somewhere between your shoulder blades, or that familiar nagging lower back, but it can lead to more serious problems, such as a slipped disc, if left unchecked.

If you have persistent back discomfort or pain your first stop is a sports physiotherapist who can diagnose and treat the exact nature of the problem. It's wise to do this before embarking on any back exercises, be it in the gym or on a yoga mat.

THE ROUTE TO A PAIN-FREE BACK

STRENGTHEN AND STRETCH FOR A HEALTHY BACK

The yoga route to a healthy, pain-free back is twofold: strengthening and stretching. On the strength side, well-conditioned back muscles will cope better with the strain of cycling, especially if they are targeted to potentially weaker areas.

This is especially the case if dropping low onto the handlebars: a posture that demands supreme strength at both the lower and upper ends of your spine. The aero tuck sequence in Chapter 8 (page 142) is designed specifically to reinforce this area, while also bolstering your back extensors.

LET THE ABS SHARE THE STRAIN

Strong abdominals are also crucial for sharing the load, and thereby reducing the chance of back problems. Cyclists with highly developed back muscles and weak abdominals risk pulling the spine out of alignment.

A strong core will bolster the entire torso, reducing the chances of back injury and build strength for climbing or sprinting. See Chapter 8 for a range of postures to strengthen the abdominals, from the deep layer transverse to the stabilising obliques.

MAINTAINING YOUR BACK'S RANGE OF MOTION

Keeping your back supple is as important as keeping it strong. The spine is designed to rotate, side-bend (lateral flexion), forward-bend (flexion) and backbend (extension). Out of all these movements the average person spends most of their time in a position of slight flexion, especially if they have a desk job or drive frequently. Even relaxing on the sofa, your back is rounded (a compromise is to sit on the sofa cross-legged, with a straight back!).

Throw in some intense hours spent on the bike and it's no surprise that back pain is such a common cycling complaint. The spine is simply spending a disproportionate amount of time fixed at one end of its range. The intervertebral discs are compressed, muscles and ligaments strained.

Easing a healthy spine into gentle extension through backbends will release some of this tension and lengthen shortened muscles, like your pecs, at the front of the body. Throw in other ranges of motion, such as lateral flexion (side-bending) or rotations to keep the whole spine mobile.

If your back aches, don't confine stretching purely to your back as problems here can often be traced back to limited hip mobility. Tight hip flexors (and hamstrings) pull your pelvis into a posterior tilt. This forces your lower back to round more so you can maintain an aerodynamic stance. Tight glutes are another common culprit when it comes to lower back discomfort. Refer to Chapter 4 for ways to keep all these areas supple, or try an all-round solution: the cyclist's sun salutation in Chapter 9 (page 156).

Finally, many of these spinal movements have the added benefit of aiding deep breathing by unlocking tension in your torso. Don't think of them as a chore: to ease into a gentle backbend feels fantastic after a ride, so explore and enjoy.

POST-RIDE TENSION RELEASERS

These yoga postures and sequences will gently ease tightness out of your back – particularly your lower (or lumbar) spine – as part of a recovery routine. This makes them ideal post-ride back exercises when you are tired. They are also good foundation sequences to start experimenting with backbends, especially if your back is not accustomed to extension.

Low back massage

This is a simple way to unlock post-ride tightness in your lower back.

Lie on your back and hug your legs in towards your abdomen. Keep your head on the floor but if your head tilts back, place a cushion or block underneath it.

Step 1: Massage your lower back by hugging your legs in tightly and rocking from side to side, or keeping your knees together and move them in a slow, circular motion.

Step 2: Inhale and move your legs away from your abdomen until your arms straighten. Exhale and draw them into your abdomen. Repeat four times.

Post-ride releaser

The perfect post-ride posture; it releases a tight lower back and provides a light stretch for tight hamstrings and glutes. Lie on your back and hug your left leg into your abdomen. Place both hands on your knee and hug your leg closer. At the same time, press the straight left leg deeper into the floor and point your left toes to the ceiling. Repeat with the other leg.

Full body stretch

To lengthen a compressed back simply collapse on the floor, sweep your arms up and reach to the back of the room. Stretch your fingertips away and point your toes or push your heels in the opposite direction.

DYNAMIC STRETCH

Start with your arms by the sides, palms facing downwards. On an inhalation sweep both arms up and back and reach towards the back of the room.

On an exhalation relax your hands and sweep your arms back down to your sides. Syncronize the breath and movement. Repeat four times.

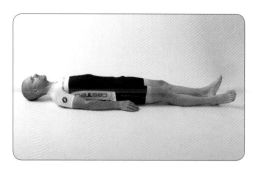

LATERAL STRETCH

Sweep both arms up and back. Take hold of your left wrist with your right hand and draw it over to your right so the body bends in that direction. Cross the left ankle over the right to target the outer hip and iliotibial band. Return to the centre and repeat on the other side.

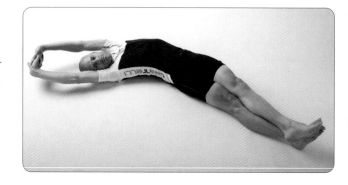

Child's pose

Child's pose provides a gentle stretch by allowing the whole back to relax. Extended child's pose also stretches your upper back and shoulders. If kneeling is uncomfortable, opt for low back massage instead (see page 91). A cushion placed between your heels and hips (or under the forehead, if your head doesn't reach the floor) will make the pose more accessible and comfortable.

BASIC CHILD'S POSE

Sit in a kneeling position. Inhale, and as you exhale, fold forwards until the forehead rests on the floor. Relax your arms by the sides, palms face up. Breathe deeply through your nose, feeling your back muscles expanding as you breathe in and releasing as you breathe out. Stay for five to ten breaths.

EXTENDED CHILD

Combine a back releaser with a deep shoulder stretch by straightening your arms in front and inching your fingers to the top of the mat. Then press your palms into the mat and draw your hips backwards to lengthen and decompress the spine. Stay for five to ten breaths.

LATERAL STRETCH CHILD

From extended child, raise the forehead off the floor and walk your hands to your left. Ensure they are still roughly shoulder-width apart. Press your palms into the floor and relax your head. Stay for five to ten breaths, then repeat the stretch walking your hands to your right.

EXTENDED CHILD
WITH HIP STRETCH

Repeat extended child, taking your knees to the edges of the mat. This will provide a stretch for your hips and inner thighs.

CHAIR VERSION

If kneeling is uncomfortable, the back lengthening benefits of the child's pose are easily gained sitting in a chair. Simply sit tall in a chair, with your feet hip-distance apart. Tuck your chin in and slowly round your back letting your arms hang heavily to stretch your shoulders. Continue to curl downwards. When you can go no further, close your eyes and completely relax the whole back. Stay for five to ten breaths, then reverse the process to rise up, raising your head up last.

Half dog

Half dog lengthens and decompresses the spine, and stretches your shoulders and chest muscles, making it a satisfying stretch for cyclists. However, it can feel intense, so if your back or shoulders are tight enter and exit gradually.

From all fours, lower the forehead towards the floor, but keep your hips raised so that your legs form a right-angle shape. Fold the arms and rest the head on the back of the top hand. If this feels OK, start to stretch your arms out in front and parallel. To deepen the stretch inch your fingers further away, press into your palms and draw your hips backwards. Stay for five breaths and exit slowly.

Roll downs (and rolls ups)

Roll downs (and roll up) use the weight of the dangling arms and gravity to stretch your back, section by section. If your back is healthy and strong, come all the way into a forward-bend, dropping your fingertips to the floor. For a modified version, perform seated in a chair (see chair version of child's pose on page 94). Roll down in slow motion, breathe slowly through your nose, and – if possible – keep your eyes closed.

Stand with your feet hip-distance apart with your arms relaxed by your sides. Bend your knees a little, draw your abdomen in and tuck your tailbone under. Draw your chin in and tip your head forwards. Then start to flex the back in slow motion so the spine gradually curves. Let your arms dangle freely. Either stop halfway down to focus on your upper back and allow your arms to hang, or continue curling down until your fingertips touch the floor. Your knees are bent throughout. Either drop down into a squat or roll up by performing the exercise in reverse.

Decompressing the spine

These postures decompress the spine and stretch your shoulders after a long ride, using a doorframe and wall or kitchen counter.

DOORFRAME HANG

This simple spinal decompression exercise deserves a section to itself for the pure relief it provides to a back that's been bent over a bike for hours. Aside from lengthening tight back extensors, it will also help reduce pressure on the intervertebral discs. You may already do it instinctively after a ride.

Grip the doorframe (a strong one!) with both hands, ensuring your arms are straight, then bend your knees until you begin to feel the muscle fibres of your arms, shoulders and back lengthening. If a doorframe is too weak, a pull-up bar in a gym will take the weight. It's tempting to lift your feet completely off the floor so the whole body is suspended, but for an optimum stretch to the spine, keep them grounded with your legs bent, so your back is straight.

KITCHEN COUNTER STRETCH

This is a gem for time-crunched cyclists as it is a great tension-releaser for your back, as well as stretching tight chest muscles and shoulders. It can also be done against a wall or using a chair, but kitchen counters tend to be the right height to really settle into the stretch. Place your palms on the kitchen surface shoulder-width apart, or wider if your upper body is particularly stiff. Walk backwards until the body folds into a 90° position. Move your feet hip-width apart. Drop your head in line with your torso and tuck your tailbone under so you are not dipping in your lower back. Stay for thirty to sixty seconds. Sway your hips to your right, then to your left to work further into the sides of your torso. Exit slowly and carefully, and perform some shoulder rolls.

BACKBENDS

If the word 'backbend' conjures up images of contortionists or Olympic gymnasts don't worry, as none of the postures in this section are advanced. Simply put: the aim of a backbend for cyclists is to allow a spine that has spent hours on the road in flexion to gently extend. This keeps your back supple, comfortable and less prone to injury. It also feels pretty good.

The function of backbends

1 To release tension, particularly in the extensor muscles that hold the spine in the cycling posture.
2 To stretch your pectoralis muscles that can become shortened over time during cycling by opening up the front of the body.
3 To retract, or draw back, your shoulders to prevent rounded shoulders and maintain good off bike posture.
4 To make the muscles of your torso more supple to facilitate deeper breathing, allowing your ribcage to expand more freely while riding (see Chapter 3).
5 To occasionally stretch other anterior areas of the body, including your hip flexors and quads. 'Bow', (see page 103) for example, stretches your pecs, hip flexors and quads, while also drawing back your shoulders. It flips the cycling position into reverse by opening up the entire front body.

STANDING BACKBEND

This posture is a good one to learn how to apply the principles in the box above. The block keeps your leg muscles engaged in order to focus more on the backbend and strengthens your inner thighs.

Take a yoga block or cushion and place it between your thighs. Contract your thighs to squeeze the block and continue to keep your leg muscles engaged. Now bring your attention to your back. Tuck your tailbone under to minimise your lower back arch and take your arms out at shoulder-height. Come into a gentle backbend, ensuring that you are extending evenly up the spine, and not just in the more mobile lower back and cervical or neck vertebrae. Lift your chin a little and draw your arms back to stretch your shoulders and chest. Breathe slowly through your nose for five to ten breaths. Gradually straighten up and counter pose either by performing a gentle standing forward-bend with your knees bent or dropping down into a squat.

Backbending safely

As beneficial as it may be to extend the spine, our bodies spend a lot of time flexed forwards so backbends need to be approached gradually. If your main sport is cycling, you have a desk job and drive a lot, the chances are your back is stiff. This is fine and normal. See a sports physiotherapist before embarking on backbends if you have any concerns about prolonged or persistent backache or pain either during rides or while sitting or standing. Otherwise, read the 'rules' in the box below and enjoy trying out some of the postures that follow.

How to backbend

Keep your tailbone tucked under: this helps to protect your lower back in backbends.

Don't over-extend your lower back: Your back bends easily in the lumbar region where the discs are larger – one-third of the thickness of the vertebral bodies. Move higher to the thoracic region or mid-back and the discs are only one-sixth that of the bodies. They also attach to the ribs, and this further restricts movement. Therefore, to gain an even backbend, slightly limit extension in your lower back and neck, and focus on the mid-back.

Don't drop your head back: The average head weighs 10 pounds, and your neck is a delicate area of the body, so avoid this unnecessary compression. Cyclists also spend a lot of time with the neck extended so further extension is not recommended. Instructions vary according to the backbend, but a good principle is to keep your neck long and continue the line of the spine into the cervical, or neck, vertebrae. This means, for example, in the standing backbend that your head will be just slightly tilted up instead of completely dropped back.

Keep the breath flowing: Backbends feel a little strange at first, but don't hold the breath. Instead keep it moving smoothly in and out of your nose. This will engage the body's calming parasympathetic nervous system and allow you to relax and explore spinal extension more freely.

Counterpose: 'Counterposing' in this context simply means following a backbend with a forward-bend. Yoga is all about creating balance in the body. Performing lots of backbends could create tension in your lower back so always follow a backbend with the recommended forward-bend.

Prone backbends

SPHINX

Sphinx is a useful prone backbend to start with as it is gentle and will provide feedback on the levels of tightness in your chest and abdomen, as well as your lower back.

Lie on your front. Position your arms so that your elbows are stacked under your shoulders and the forearms are parallel in a 90° position. There should be no strain in your arms. Tuck your tailbone under to lessen the pressure on your lower back. Slide your shoulder blades down your back and raise your head a little, but keep the back of your neck long. Stay for five breaths. Ease slowly back to all fours and round your back. Sink back onto your heels as in extended child (see page 93).

COBRA

If sphinx is a deep enough backbend for you stick with it. To extend the spine a little more, and strengthen your arms try cobra.

Here are three versions: strength cobra largely strengthens your back, basic cobra extends your back while striking cobra provides the deepest spinal extension. The last two also build arm strength. Monitor your lower back carefully, only advancing the cobra variation if there is no discomfort.

Strength cobra: Slide your hands underneath your shoulders, keeping your elbows tucked into the sides. Lift your upper body on an inhalation using only your back muscles to elevate. Resist the urge to push into your palms (check this by lifting your palms an inch off the floor) so your back is doing the work. Keep the back of your neck long looking only to the top of the mat. Stay for five to ten slow breaths and lower down. Ease slowly back onto all fours and round your back. Sink back in extended child.

Basic cobra: Slide your hands underneath your shoulders, keeping your elbows tucked into the sides. Lift your upper back on an inhalation, as before, but this time gain an extra inch by pressing your palms into the floor and using your arms to elevate your upper body. Tuck your tailbone under and slide your shoulder blades down. Stay for five breaths and lower down. Ease onto all fours and sit back in extended child.

Striking cobra: Repeat Cobra but – only if your lower back is comfortable – straighten your arms a little to raise your upper body higher. Keep tucking your tailbone under to lessen the pressure on your lower back. Stay for three to five breaths and lower down. Ease onto all fours and sit back in child, sweeping your arms by the sides and rocking side-to-side across the forehead.

SNAKE

Snake strengthens your back extensors while really opening up your chest and shoulders so is ideal for cyclists. It also works the glutes if you raise your legs too. Can't reach to interlace your fingers? Keep your arms parallel and spread your fingers wide.

Lie down on your front. Rest your forehead on the floor and move your arms by the sides. Interlace your fingers and draw your shoulders back. Lift your upper body on an inhalation and remain here for five breaths ensuring the back of your neck is long. On an exhalation, lower down and either sit slowly back in child or repeat, raising your upper body and legs.

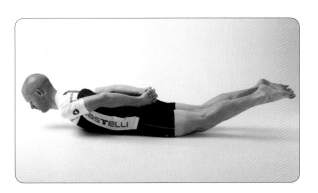

Five steps to bow pose

Bow completely flips the flexed riding position into extension, making it a must-have for cyclists. It lengthens the entire front of the body, including your quads, hip flexors and shoulders. The body requires a little warming up to reach the final bow posture, so practise the steps sequentially and have a strap (yoga strap or old tie) handy.

STEP 1: SHOULDER WARM-UPS

Sit in a kneeling position and perform some slow shoulder rolls. Then drop your hands on to your shoulders and make circles with your elbows. Finally, interlace your fingers behind you and lift your arms up, keeping your back straight while breathing slowly.

STEP 2: QUAD WARM-UPS

From kneeling, take your hands behind your back, fingers pointing to the back of the room to open your shoulders. As you inhale lift your hips up to stretch your quads. As you exhale, lower down. If this is too strong, try a half version, with one leg still in a kneeling position. Hold the pose up statically, keeping your chin tucked in, for four breaths.

STEP 3: STRINGLESS BOW

Lie on your front with your arms by your sides, palms face down. Bend your legs so they form a 90° angle. Lift your upper body on an inhalation, but keep your thighs on the floor. Spread your fingers and take five breaths. Lower down and sink slowly back in child's pose.

STEP 4: STRAP BOW

Loop the strap around your ankles and return to the prone position. Bend your legs again and lift your upper body on an inhalation. Flex your feet to hold the strap in place. On an inhalation, rise up, walking your hands down the strap. Hold for up to five breaths, keeping your tailbone tucked under and the back of your neck long.

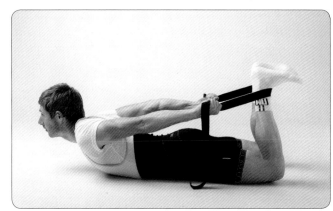

STEP 5: FULL BOW

This time, reach back and see if your ankles are close enough to hold. Don't let your knees go wide – if your feet are too far away lower down and repeat with the strap. Hold the posture for up to five breaths, keeping your tailbone tucked under and the back of your neck long. Notice how your upper body rises as your lungs fill and lower as they empty. Lower down and sink slowly back into child's pose.

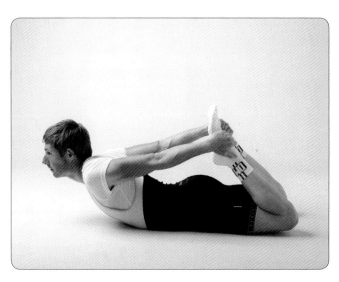

SIDE-BENDS

Side-bends have two benefits for cyclists: to strengthen and stretch the oblique abdominals at the sides of the waist, and to release tension in your torso, waist and side of your hips. The obliques and lateral hip muscles form a key 'stilling and stabilising' role as you ride. All also stretch the iliotibial band.

STANDING SIDE-BEND

Stand with your feet hip-distance apart. Interlace your fingers and turn your palms towards the ceiling. On an inhalation, lift a little higher, and on an exhalation tip to your right side. Try not to lean forwards or backwards to perform a pure side-bend. Stay for five breaths keeping your abdomen drawn in and tailbone tucked under. Return to the centre and exhale over to your left side. This can also be performed sitting.

TRIANGLE

Triangle shifts cyclists out of a linear motion and into a lateral stretch that can be felt from ankle to fingertips, making it a valuable posture. This includes the iliotibial band: a tight band of connective tissue on your outer thigh that can be aggravated by the repetitive action of pedalling. The freestanding triangle that follows will improve balance and bolster the obliques, or try the wall triangle variation to relax into an intense stretch.

Stand in the middle of the mat and step your feet wide. Turn your back foot 45° in while the front foot points straight ahead. Engage your leg muscles. On an inhalation, sweep both arms up in line with your shoulders. As you exhale lean forwards as if reaching, then lower the front hand down and rest it lightly on your thigh. Raise your back arm up and reach to the ceiling. Spread your fingers and try to lift out of the posture by engaging your abs to keep the weight out of your lower hand.

To move deeper into triangle step the legs wider drop the top arm over by the ear into extended triangle. Remain looking straight ahead. Stay for five to ten breaths. To exit, place the top hand on your hip, bend the front knee and slowly rise up. Relax your arms and roll your shoulders. Repeat on the other side.

ABOVE: *Extended triangle*

WALL TRIANGLE

Repeat triangle but with your back to the wall, close enough to rest your buttocks, shoulders and back of your head on its surface. As you exhale slide into triangle, as above but this time lean into the wall. Experiment with your arm position, first taking your arm up and maybe over by the ear. Close your eyes and take five to ten breaths feeling the intensity of the stretch. Exit slowly, placing your hand on your hip and bending the front leg to rise up. Relax your arms and roll your shoulders. Repeat on the other side.

ROTATIONS

Our last spinal movement is rotation. Unlike golfers or tennis players, cyclists don't need or want to twist – just the opposite. But these postures are a useful way of releasing torso tension, especially in the middle or thoracic region, which can be difficult to stretch. The seated and lying twists also provide a bonus glute stretch, and in some cases a piriformis stretch. A last reminder: if you encounter any problems with your lower back, choose the first few gentle options and enter the twist with care. *Avoid twists if you have a diagnosed slipped disc.*

How to rotate

1 **Lengthen the spine first:** a compressed spine can't rotate properly, so first lengthen the spine by sitting or standing tall with a straight back. Imagine a thread lifting from the crown of your head, like a puppet.
2 **Work with the breath:** As you lengthen, take a deep inhalation. As you rotate, let this breath out slowly. Once in the twist continue this process on a smaller scale, lifting on the in-breath and rotating on the out-breath.
3 **Use props:** Tight hips will inhibit a good spinal twist so in seated twists first get comfortable by sitting on the edge of a yoga block or cushion. This also creates a straighter, taller spine. In the lying twists, place a block under your knees if they are hovering off the floor.
4 **Rotate evenly:** Because the lumbar vertebrae are more mobile, they will twist more easily than the thoracic vertebrae in the mid-back. This is because the thoracic discs are smaller and some movement is constricted by the ribcage. The solution to rotating evenly up the length of the spine is to begin twisting at your lower back, then stop and continue the twist up through the thoracic spine. Leave the final section of the twist to the more mobile cervical neck vertebrae.

STANDING TWIST

A simple way to begin to increase range of motion in twists is to do a standing rotation. Just stand with your feet hip-distance apart and fold your arms. Inhale, and as you exhale, rotate to your left. Inhale back to the centre and repeat to your right.

TENSION-RELEASING TWIST

To release upper body tension post-ride, repeat Standing Twist but relax the arms and let them swing freely as you rotate from side to side. Ensure the knees are slightly bent. Let the head turn with the body.

ALL FOURS TWIST

Begin on all fours, gazing down at the floor. As you inhale, sweep your right arm up towards the ceiling, keeping your eyes fixed on your right hand. As you exhale, return your arm and repeat to your left side. Repeat four times each side, aiming for a little more rotation each time.

SEATED TWIST

Sit with your legs stretched out in front. If it's hard to maintain a tall back, sit on the edge of a block or cushion. Bend your left leg and step your foot over your right thigh. Before you rotate, hold onto your left shin with both hands and lengthen the spine. Wrap your right arm around your left thigh and drop your left fingertips to the floor behind you. Inhale, and as you exhale, begin to rotate to your left in sections: lumbar spine, thoracic spine, shoulders and finally head. Remain here for five breaths. Continue to rotate a little further with each breath. Return to face front and repeat on the other side.

ADVANCED SEATED TWIST

If your hips are supple enough try advancing the twist. This pose targets the ITB, piriformis as well as stretching the erector spinae muscles in your upper body. From the start position with your legs out in front, bend your left leg and step your foot over your right thigh as before. Now lean to your right and bend your right leg so that your heel of your right foot is next to your left buttock. Try to level your hips (place a cushion under one hip if it is lower). Wrap your right arm around your left thigh and drop your left fingertips to the floor behind you. Inhale, and as you exhale, rotate to your left. Hold the pose for five breaths. Return to face front and repeat on the other side.

Lying twists

Lying twists can be deeply relaxing or a challenging stretch, depending on the variation. Begin with the gentlest bent-legged rotation, but have a strap nearby if you feel like advancing the pose by straightening your legs. You may also need to place blocks or cushions under your knees.

LYING TWIST 1: BENT LEGS

Lie on your back with your legs bent, hip-distance apart, and feet on the floor. Take your arms shoulder-height, palms facing upward. Breathe in, and as you breathe out, lower your knees down to the floor on your right side. Place a block or cushion under your knees if they don't reach the floor. Rotate your head in the opposite direction and relax. Close your eyes and stay for up to a minute. To exit, draw your legs back to the centre and hug them into your abdomen. Repeat on the other side.

LYING TWIST 2: STRAIGHT LEGS

Have a strap nearby. Repeat lying twist 1, but when your legs touch the floor, try straightening them. If your hamstrings are tight, loop the strap around the soles of both feet. Hold both parts of the strap in your right hand and extend your left arm along the floor. Rotate your head to your left and remain here for up to a minute. To exit, first release the strap, draw your abdomen in, bend your legs and return to the centre. Repeat on the other side.

07

CYCLISTS' POWER YOGA

❛ I find a lot of balance in doing other less cardio-driven workouts that help me with body control and alignment. Learning where your body is tight, inflexible or less responsive is powerful. Yoga and gym work are exceptional training tools that give you strength, balance and personal body awareness that you just won't find swimming, biking and running. There's nothing more powerful than feeling that you have control over your body! ❜

Chris McCormack, two-time Ironman World Champion,
*Triathlete Europe magazine***, June 2012**

Greater flexibility is what attracts sports people to yoga, but anyone who has felt his muscles shake holding 'plank' or 'warrior 1' will testify that it also builds strength. Yoga's strength-building power postures won't, however, add bulk. For cyclists keen to create lean muscle fibres to stay lightweight on the bike, this makes it a great strength option.

The yogic theory is that a healthy body is both supple and strong. It is powerful, yet pliable – not so supple that the joints are weakened and muscles are unable to perform their stabilising and driving role; not so strong and stiff that range of motion is lost and injury risked.

In a cyclist's case this means a lower back that is flexible enough to lower effortlessly into an aerodynamic stance, but also has the resilience to maintain this position in comfort for as long as you want to ride. It means hamstrings, quads and calves strong and supple enough to apply maximum force to the pedals by moving your legs through a greater range of motion.

STRENGTH WITHOUT BULK

Powerful but pliable

Yoga poses produce lean muscle due to their unique ability to build strength while also lengthening. Every posture in this chapter works and stretches the body simultaneously. Unlike gym equipment that tends to isolate muscle groups, a single yoga posture may be strengthening many groups at the same time. Therefore, while a posture may be classified in this chapter as 'strengthening for your quads', the reality of exactly what's going on under the skin is far more complicated.

Take side angle pose (page 121). It lengthens the muscles in the entire side of the body and teases tension out of your hips, particularly gluteus medius. On the strength side, the side angle pose primarily works the obliques, and the abdominal muscles at the side of the waist that facilitate upper body stillness on the bike, but is also challenging the quads and hamstrings of your bent leg.

The postures in this chapter, therefore, may focus on building strength in your quads or hamstrings, but are essentially whole-body exercises: they build strength, they stretch and – if slow, nasal deep breathing is used – will also have a calming effect on the mind.

Achieving whole-body balanced strength, by easing the body through twists, backbends, side-bends and lunges, will make you strong for cycling. It will also free you up to play football, go for a run or sit at a desk without cursing your restrictive hamstrings, hips or back.

Correcting cycling imbalances

Balanced strength is important for cyclists as, due to its repetitive, linear nature, the sport can create muscular imbalances. Take your legs: most riders have (and need) strong quads, but possess significantly weaker hamstrings and inner thigh muscles.

This can lead to potential problems as your kneecap is pulled out of alignment. Stick pose in this chapter tackles this imbalance by strengthening your innermost quad, or vastus medialis, which is sometimes called the 'teardrop' muscle due to its shape.

Because cyclists train only in the sagittal (or forward-moving) plane, lateral strength is also frequently lacking. Therefore, this chapter includes a section on side-bends to address this potential weakness.

Building lower leg strength

Your lower legs, ankles and feet are strengthened in this chapter through a range of standing balances. These postures can also help cyclists improve their sense of on-bike balance. This, combined with a strong core, enables a rider to focus more on pedalling efficiency.

Balances don't need to be complicated. Rising up onto the balls of your feet is a simple way to improve it and strengthen the calf muscles at the same time.

Static strength or fast flow?

Muscular strength is created in two ways, depending on whether you hold the postures statically, or practise them within a dynamic faster sequence or 'flow'.

The first method is isometric strength training, whereby the muscle length does not change during contraction. You might hold a posture for five to ten breaths, or longer.

Moving the body dynamically in and out of postures is isotonic. The muscles alternately contract and release as you move through the sequence. To put it in a sporting context: rock climbing or rifle shooting is isometric, while cycling or running is isotonic.

Both are valid ways to strengthen. Stronger flowing styles of yoga like ashtanga or power yoga are become increasingly popular in gyms. Classes are likely to attract sportspeople who feel the strenuous postures and fast pace are more akin to the cardiovascular workout they love than straight static stretching.

Sequences tend to feature a high number of the strength-building postures shown in this chapter, like dog and the warrior postures, which are sequenced in a dynamic stretching and strengthening routine known as a sun salutation (detailed in Chapter 9; see page 156).

However, moving fast has its downsides. Injuries in yoga, especially involving the rotator cuff or lower back, are not unknown. Precision can get lost in the bid to keep up with the rest of the class. Therefore, try the postures in this chapter statically first to ensure correct alignment (which can be just as tough) and, once mastered, go to Chapter 9 and choose a strengthening flow or invent your own.

Don't tackle these power poses post-ride if it's been a heavy session as the muscles are already tired. Opt instead for a handful of post-ride muscle lengthening postures in this book (see Chapter 11).

The best time to think about a stronger yoga practice is after a light ride or a non-cycling day. If you are a serious athlete the off-season is an ideal time to practise once or twice a week. Weave sessions into your strength and conditioning programme to return supple and strong in spring.

THE QUAD STRENGTHENERS

CHAIR POSE

The Sanskrit term for chair pose translates into English as 'fierce pose', and after a few minutes in it you'll feel the intensity in your quads, but your hamstrings and glutes are working too. It's the yoga equivalent of using a gym leg press machine. Experiment with your arms: if your shoulders are already sore from riding take your hands behind your head or to your hips. As with all the stronger poses, breathe slowly through your nose.

Targets: Quads, hamstrings, glutes and triceps. Stretches your calves.

Bike benefits: Your quads and glutes assist the downward pedal stroke.

Method: Stand with your feet together. On an inhale sweep both arms up alongside the ears or interlace your hands behind your head. On an exhalation bend your knees and sink into a high squat. Tuck your tailbone under. Gaze ahead. Take five to ten slow breaths.

Modify: Knee injury: remain in a high squat, hands on hips. Sore upper back: place your hands on your hips.

Advance: Sink lower.

BLOCK CHAIR

Targets: The adductors and vastus medialis, your innermost quads.

Bike benefits: Cycling tends to overwork your outer thighs which can cause a muscular imbalance around your knee joint. Squeezing a block between the thighs, either in chair or in a 90-degree leg position resting the back against the wall can help redress this imbalance. A small physio ball or cushion can be used as a block substitute.

Method: Prepare to perform chair, but this time place a yoga block or cushion between your thighs and squeeze it using inner thigh strength. Come into chair and maintain this block pressure for five to ten slow breaths.

Modify: Knee injury: remain in a higher squat, hands on hips.

TWISTING CHAIR

Targets: Glutes, hamstrings and quads. Stretches your back.

Bike benefits: Similar to chair pose, but twisting chair also releases tension in the back muscles that maintain riding posture.

Method: Prepare to perform chair, but join your palms at chest-height. On an exhale sink into chair then twist your upper body to your left keeping your knees level. To come deeper into the pose, sink low enough to anchor your right elbow to the outside of your left knee. This will give you the leverage to twist further. Stay for five breaths and slowly rise up. Repeat on the other side.

Modify: Back or knee issues: perform the twist in a higher squat.

Advance: As you twist to your left drop your right fingertips to the floor by your outer edge of your left foot and extend your left arm to the ceiling.

The lunges

The postures in this section are variations of a basic yoga lunge called warrior 1. As the name implies, these are serious strength-building poses – working your quads and glutes. But stay long enough to deeply stretch your hip flexors and calf muscles of your back leg.

WARRIOR 1

Targets: Quads, hamstrings and adductors of your front leg. Stretches hip flexors and calf of your back leg.

Bike benefits: Strong quads and hamstrings create a powerful pedal stroke and the explosive power to accelerate. Restores your calf muscles back to their resting length.

Method: From the middle of your mat take a good step back with your left foot. Turn your back foot slightly out and bend the front knee until it is behind or stacked over your ankle. Take your hands to your hips or front of your thigh. Stay for five to ten breaths. Keep working your back heel to the floor.

Modification: Knee problems: perform a higher lunge and ensure the knee of your front leg is behind or stacked above your ankle.

Advance: Sink lower and deepen your backbend, sweep the arms up into a 'v' shape.

LEANING LUNGE

Targets: Increases the strength work for your quads and hamstrings. Stretches hip flexor and calf muscle of your back leg, and chest (especially if your hands are interlaced behind your back).

Bike benefits: As with warrior 1, but these two leaning variations both strengthen, then stretch, your upper back and shoulders.

Method: From the middle of the mat take a good step back with your left foot. Rise onto the ball of your back foot and bend the front knee until it is behind or stacked over your ankle. Lean your torso slightly over your leg. There are two options from here. Arms forwards: draw in your abdomen and reach both arms forwards and parallel. Spread your fingers. Stay for five to ten breaths. Arms back: sweep your arms back and – if your shoulders allow – interlace your fingers. Stay for a further five to ten breaths.

Modification: Knee problems: perform a higher lunge to lessen the work of your quads.

Advance: Shuffle your back foot further back until the front thigh is parallel with the floor.

TWISTING LUNGE

Targets: Quads, hamstrings and glutes.

Stretches: hip flexors and calf of your back leg. Releases tension in your back, torso and shoulders.

Bike benefits: As with warrior 1, but creates a supple torso to ease tension and facilitate deeper breathing while cycling.

Method: Drop both hands to the floor either side of your foot as if performing a high runner's lunge. As you inhale sweep your right arm up to the ceiling, turning your head to gaze at your hand. Exhale as you return your arm by the side. Repeat with the other arm, moving from side to side with the breath. Repeat five times each side.

Modification: Tired legs: drop your back knee to the floor and perform a lower version.

Lunging backbend

No time to stretch? This backbend is a great timesaver for cyclists. It lengthens your upper quads, hip flexors, pecs and shoulders. It also strengthens your neck extensors if you gently push your head into your hands, and challenges the sense of balance.

STEP 1

Start on all fours. Step your right foot up in between your hands. Rise onto the ball of your back foot. Draw your abdomen in and lift your torso so it is stacked over your hips. Start by placing both hands on the front thigh and focus on your legs. You are looking for a deep (but not painful) stretch in your upper quad and top of your back thigh. To deepen the stretch, sink lower, to lessen: rise up. Now tuck your tailbone under to lessen the lumbar curve and start to lean into a gentle backbend. Breathe slowly through your nose. If you feel unsteady remain here.

STEP 2

To move further into the pose sweep both arms up and interlace your fingers behind your head. Try to relax your head into your hands and keep your shoulders down. Now focus on stretching your pecs and shoulders by drawing your elbows back, just out of the line of vision. Hold the posture for five to ten breaths. Ease out slowly and repeat on the other side. End by sinking into child's pose.

SEATED INNER QUAD STRENGTHENER

Targets: Vastus medialis and back. Stretches your hamstrings.

Bike benefits: Cycling works your outermost quads leaving the medial, or innermost, quads comparatively weak. This imbalance can lead to knee problems.

Method: Sit with your legs stretched out in front and close together. Straighten your back by lifting from the crown of your head and pressing your palms lightly into the floor. To activate the inner quads push your knees into the floor and hold for twenty seconds, breathing steadily. Repeat four times.

THE LATERAL STRENGTHENERS

Because cyclists move in a linear motion, your hip and leg muscles responsible for sideways or lateral movement, can become weakened. These lateral strengtheners work your outer and inner thighs and muscles of the side torso like the oblique abdominals. Also, these side-to-side postures give your hips a good stretch, releasing the tension that accumulates from holding your thighs steady while you pedal.

HORSE

Targets: Glutes, inner and outer thighs. Stretches your hips and inner thighs.

Bike benefits: Glute power while releasing hip tension.

Method: Turn sideways if you are on a mat. Step your feet wide and turn your toes slightly out. Place your hands on your hips. Tuck your tailbone under so your lower back is not arching. Inhale. On an exhalation bend your knees and come into a high squat so your knees track with the second toe. Don't let your knees fall inwards. Take five to ten slow breaths. Rise up and heel-toe your feet back together.

Modification: Knee issues: perform a higher squat.

Advance: For a deeper squat bring your palms together. On every exhale sink lower until you are close to the floor then work your way back up to the start position.

DYNAMIC SIDE LUNGE

Targets: Strengthens and stretches the adductors located in your inner thighs. Works your quads, hamstrings and glutes. Releases hip tension.

Bike benefits: Weak inner thighs combined with overdeveloped quads can lead to knee problems for cyclists. This side lunge creates lateral strength to redress this imbalance.

Method: From horse, step your feet wider but keep your toes turned out. Place your hands on your thighs. Inhale and on an exhale shift your weight over as you move into a side lunge.

Check your alignment: Your knee should slide in line with your second or third toe. Inhale back to the centre and exhale to the other side. Repeat five times each side.

Modification: Knee issues: Come into a higher lunge.

WARRIOR 2

Targets: Quads and hamstrings of front leg. Stretches hip flexors, adductors and calf of back leg.

Bike benefits: Aside from strengthening the front leg, warrior 2 shifts the cyclist's body into a lateral plane, creating balanced strength.

Method: Turn sideways on the mat and step your feet wide apart. Turn your left toes out 90° and right foot in 45°. Bend your front leg ensuring your knee is behind or stacked over your ankle. To increase the intensity slide your back foot further back and sink lower. Keeping your torso stacked over your hips raise both arms up to shoulder height, palms face down. Imagine that you are being pulled in opposite directions by your fingertips. Keep your shoulders relaxed and low. Gaze beyond the front hand and take five to ten deep breaths.

Modify: Knee issues: don't sink too low.

Advance: Shuffle your back foot away to lower the stance until the front thigh is parallel to the ground.

SIDE ANGLE POSE

Targets: Quads and hamstrings of front leg and obliques. Stretches the entire side of the body.

Bike benefits: Creates balanced hamstring/ quad strength for pedalling power, and reinforces the stabilising obliques to minimise torso movement.

Method: Inhale in warrior 2 and, as you exhale, bend your left leg and lean into a side-bend, resting your left forearm lightly on the front thigh. Less weight resting on your thigh means the obliques are forced to work harder. Sweep your right arm just by your right ear so that there is a straight line running from your back heel to the top fingertips. Stay for five breaths.

Modify: Knee issues: perform a higher version with a narrower stance. If the top arm is aching, rest your hand on your hip.

Advance: To advance the pose drop your left fingertips down to the outside of your left foot and activate your left inner thigh by pushing your knee into your elbow to brace your legs. Look ahead or gaze up. Slowly exit the pose and switch sides.

REVERSE WARRIOR

Targets: Quads and hamstrings of front leg. Stretches hips and torso.

Bike benefits: Aside from working your quad and inner thigh of the front leg, reverse warrior keeps the muscles around your torso supple. This eases muscular tightness that can prevent deep breathing on the bike.

Method: Inhale in warrior 2. On an exhale, sweep the front arm up and reach to the ceiling as you slide your back arm down your back leg, as if performing a wide-legged tennis serve. Turn your palm to face the back of the room and take five breaths. Exit slowly and repeat on the other side.

Modify: The combined side-bend/back bend action of reverse warrior can compress your lower back. Rise up and limit your backbend.

Advance: Widen your leg stance by shuffling your back foot away until the front thigh is parallel with the floor.

FOOT AND ANKLE STRENGTHENERS

These simple standing balances will improve the sense of balance while strengthening your feet and ankles by forcing these muscles to rapidly contract and release, to steady the whole body.

CALF RAISES

Targets: Muscles of the calf, ankle and foot. Improves balance.

Bike benefits: A simple way of improving balance and working the calves (gastrocnemius and soleus). The calves contribute power to each pedal rotation.

Method: Stand with your feet hip-distance apart, arms by your side. Gaze ahead, and on an inhale rise onto your toes trying not to tip forwards or sway back. Exhale and lower.

Advance: As you rise onto your toes sweep both arms up above your head. Lower your arms as you bring your heels to the floor. Or stay on your toes for five breaths.

Cyclist's balancing sequence

Moving in slow motion from one balance to the next will challenge the core and hip stabilisers, strengthen your feet and ankles and requires good mental concentration. This series of balances also targets your hip flexors (iliopsoas: the muscles at the top of your thigh that lift your leg each time you pedal) which cyclists need to be both supple and strong.

1 HIP FLEXOR STRENGTHENER

Stand with your feet hip-distance apart and take your hands to the hips or out at shoulder height like wings. Lift your right toes, spread them wide and lower them down again to widen your base. Now shift the weight onto your right foot. Keep your hips level, slowly raise your left leg up. Keep your leg as straight as possible and point your toes to the ceiling.

2 AEROPLANE

Begin to slowly tip forwards to make the transition into aeroplane. Keep your arms shoulder-height. Extend your left leg behind you with your toes pointing down. Aim to raise your leg up in line with your torso.

3 BALANCING LEG HUG

Rise slowly up and hug your left leg into your abdomen. To really challenge your sense of balance, tuck your chin in, drop your head down and slightly round your back.

4 CYCLIST'S QUAD STRETCH

Slide your left hand down your left shin to your ankle, and draw your leg back into a standing quad stretch. Tuck your tailbone under and – if your quad allows – line up your knees. Take your right hand to your back foot too, to really open your chest and shoulders. Remain looking forwards, or tuck your chin slightly in.

❛ Cyclists tend to focus their training on a repetitive linear pedalling motion while neglecting the supporting core structure from which much of their power and coordination is centered. Through consistent training in both yoga and Pilates, I've seen improvements in functional strength in cyclists that translates into better climbing (both seated and standing), less neck, shoulder and lower back discomfort and improved skills. ❜

Thomas Chapple, elite-level US cycling coach and author of Base Building for Cyclists (VeloPress, 2006)

Many of the gymnastic-style exercises cyclists use to strengthen the core, like plank, locust or bridge, originate from yoga postures. They are functional, simple and portable, using just the body weight as resistance: no dumbbells, stability balls or expensive gym membership required.

Pick one static core pose from each section of this chapter, or link them in a core strength sequence from Chapter 9, and you will have targeted every muscle group a cyclist needs for optimum core strength.

CORE FUNCTION FOR CYCLISTS

Does 'core' mean 'abdominals' to you? Many of the exercises here do focus on the various layers of abs. But for the purpose of this chapter 'core' also covers the oft-neglected glutes and the back. These torso muscles work together to brace your upper body over the handlebars while your legs maintain a smooth and steady pedalling motion.

Six reasons to strengthen the core

1 **Creating upper body stillness:** The abdominals, particularly the internal and external obliques, located at the sides of the waist, stabilise your upper body by minimising energy-sapping side-to-side rocking. This helps riders achieve much-sought-after upper body stillness.

2 **Building power for hill climbs and sprinting:** The corset-like transversus abdominis 'splints' the abdominal wall, bracing your torso over the handlebars. Strength here provides the extra power and stability required to stand up in the saddle and pedal.

3 **Maintaining correct posture:** Strong abdominals are also crucial for correct cycling posture (see 'Ideal cycling posture' in Chapter 2 for pointers, page 28). Without this strong reinforcement the body begins to slump as you tire and your lower back and shoulders take the strain.

4 **Balancing back strength:** Serious cyclists boast highly developed back muscles from hours in the saddle due to the fact that they remain engaged for the entire ride. This works well except in riders whose abdominals are significantly weaker – a common scenario, because while cycling requires abdominal strength, it doesn't build it.

5 **Preventing back problems:** An imbalance of strength between your back and abs can lead to a host of back issues, from niggling lower backache to more serious ailments such as slipped discs, as the spine is gradually pulled out of alignment. The yoga postures in this chapter can redress this imbalance.

6 **Preventing osteoporosis:** Many of the core postures in this chapter that require you to support your own body weight, such as plank, are also good at maintaining bone density, and therefore preventing osteoporosis (literally 'porous bones'), where the bones become brittle and susceptible to fracture. A cyclist's joints are not stressed by contact with the ground in the same way that a runner's are. So if cycling is your only sport, it's crucial to include some weight-bearing postures in your strength and conditioning repertoire to avoid problems in later life.

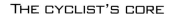

Mimicking cycling movements

Wherever possible in this chapter classic yoga postures have been tailored to suit the cyclist by mimicking the cycling stance, thereby creating targeted strengthening. For example, the section on the bridge includes a variation called cycling bridge where one foot is raised at a time to replicate the core and hip stability needed during the pedalling action. In cycling plank knees are drawn into your abdomen alternately to challenge the deep core muscles as well as your shoulders and arms.

Many postures, like plank, crow balance and cycling crunch, combine abdominal strengthening with arm, shoulders and upper back work. This is a fantastic side benefit and an ideal time-saving combination for cyclists who also want to reinforce their upper body.

The cyclist's core

- **The abdominals** comprise a deep corset-like layer – the transversus abdominis (TVA), 'six-pack' rectus abdominis and two layers of obliques at the sides of the waist. They perform various functions for cyclists. For example, rectus abdominis helps the rider sit up in the saddle and power a hill climb and is targeted in boat pose. Plank works the TVA, which is essential for maintaining posture and stability. Finally, the obliques miminise wasteful side-to-side torso rotation and create a still upper body. Build resilient obliques through side plank or lying twist.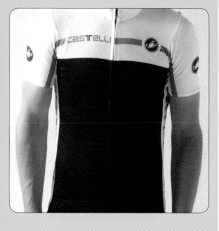

- **The glutes** or buttock muscles power and stabilise your legs. Postures that target the main gluteus maximus include basic bridge, glute plank and especially cycling bridge, a sequence which forces the glutes to work in isolation just as they do during pedalling. The smaller glute medius, at the side of your hips, is frequently overlooked but has a key role in stabilising your thigh bone. This helps channel all movement into a forward, or sagittal, plane. Access it by performing glute medius side plank with the top leg raised.

- **The back** muscles of a cyclist are likely to be strong, simply from maintaining the cycling position, this chapter features just a handful of yoga postures for backs. These highlight weaker spots such as your lower back and shoulder blades. Most, such as the locust series, perform a dual role as backbends by releasing tension in your back extensor muscles. Locust is also good for improving strength around the scapulae, especially with varied arm positions. This area needs to be extra strong to hold the body in an aero tuck position in a time trial or triathlon. See the aero tuck sequence if this is a weak area for you.

SWITCHING ON THE CORE

The following sequences focus on engaging the deep-layer TVA. These muscles may lack the glamour of the more superficial and visible 'six pack', but a solid TVA is the base for a strong core. It acts like a corset to protect your lower back and maintain posture. These gentler warm-up postures are a good starting point if the core is weak or your back is injured, but will also fire up the abs before strenuous work.

PELVIC TILT

Targets: TVA.

Bike benefits: Pelvic tilts are a simple way to engage your deep TVA and 'switch on' your abdominals for stronger work. This exercise is also an effective way of easing an aching lower back.

Method: Lie on your back. Bend your legs and place your feet on the floor, hip-width apart. On an inhalation lift the navel towards the ceiling keeping your hips on the floor to create a gap under the lumbar spine. On an exhalation press the navel into the floor to flatten your lower back. Repeat five times. Finish by hugging your legs into your abdomen.

Pelvic tilts on the bike

This exercise can easily be done on a more subtle level while riding to strengthen the TVA, and facilitate a 'flatter back' posture. It also lessens tension in your lower back and feels good after hours on the road, temporarily improving comfort levels. Pause at the traffic lights. Arch your back and tilt your pelvis out, then round your lower back and tuck the pelvis under, drawing in the deep abs. Release as you breathe out. Release as you breathe out.

CAT

Targets: TVA. Stretches entire back and shoulders.

Bike benefits: Cat is a gem for cyclists, releasing tension in the entire back, shoulders and neck post-ride, and engaging the deep core.

Method: Start on all fours. As you inhale raise your head slightly, and raise your hips, dipping in the mid-back. As you exhale, round your back, tucking your chin in and tailbone under. Push the mid-back to the ceiling and draw your belly in. Hold for a second and repeat four times.

Modify: If there is tension in the back of your neck from craning to look forwards while cycling, raise your hips but keep your head in line with your back.

TABLE TOP

Targets: TVA, glutes and hamstrings.

Bike benefits: This exercise trains cyclists to keep the core stable while moving the limbs, and improves balance.

Method: Start on all fours. Gaze downwards keeping your head in line with your torso. Engage your abdomen and slowly raise your left leg to hip height and right arm up to shoulder height in a diagonal stretch. Stay for five slow breaths then switch sides.

ADVANCED TABLE TOP

Targets: TVA, glutes, hamstrings. Stretches your neck extensors.

Bike benefits: This dynamic variation challenges cycling balance and coordination while working the deep abdominals.

Method: On an inhalation, perform table top as before. On an exhalation, round your back, bend your left leg and draw it into your abdomen. At the same time bend your right arm, take your right hand to the top of your head and draw your head in towards your abdomen too. Aim to make elbow/knee contact. As you next inhale, rise back up to table top. Repeat four times, moving from side to side.

THE PLANK SERIES

Plank is a great all-round core strengthener for cyclists, and has the added bonus of working your arms and shoulders. It targets the rectus abdominis and TVA, while the 'side' versions work the stabilising obliques. 'Low plank', with your arms at a right angle, will intensify your arm work, but is challenging as it places extra weight on the wrists which may already be stressed by hours on the bike. Look for the non-wrist modifications like forearm plank, especially if you suffer from carpal tunnel syndrome or 'handlebar palsy'.

Finally, unlike runners, cyclists place their joints under very little stress. Over time this lack of stress can lead to weaker bones and the risk of osteoporosis. Weight-bearing postures like plank will maintain bone density.

The plank rules

1 Maintain a line along the back of your body from your head to your heels. It's better to drop your knees down, drawing your abdomen in to hold onto this alignment, than sag in your lower back or lift your hips.

2 Engage your leg muscles and push your heels away so your lower limbs share the strain.

3 Wrist injury or carpal tunnel syndrome? Opt for the forearm plank.

4 Look down, not ahead, but don't let your head drop. It should continue the line of the spine.

5 Stay for five to ten slow breaths through your nose.

6 Follow planks with the extended child pose (see below), dropping your knees and slowly sitting back on your heels to stretch your shoulders and lower back. Make fists with your hands and rotate.

HIGH PLANK

Targets: TVA, rectus abdominis, arm and shoulder muscles.

Bike benefits: To create a strong, stable centre while cycling and increase arm/shoulder strength.

Method: From all fours lift your knees off the floor, ensuring the wrists are under your shoulders. Push your heels away, engaging your leg muscles to share the strain. Gaze to the floor and stay for five to ten slow breaths.

Modify: Weak core: drop your knees down, but keep your head, back and hips in line and abdomen drawn in. Wrist issues: opt for forearm plank.

LOW PLANK

Targets: Core and arms, especially triceps.

Bike benefits: The challenging 90° arm position mimics the bent-armed angle of a low sprint position or aero tuck.

Method: From high plank, bend your arms until your elbows fall in line with your torso. Stay for five to ten breaths maintaining alignment.

Modify: Drop your knees down until arm strength improves.

FOREARM PLANK

Targets: Core, upper back, shoulder and upper arm muscles.

Bike benefits: Forearm plank is a great option for cyclists as it replicates the bent armed cycling position with no weight on the wrists. Interlock your fingers for a narrower arm position to recreate your upper body position when holding onto the aero bars.

Method: Come onto the forearms, stacking your elbows under your shoulders. Make fists with your hands and keep the forearms parallel, or interlock them. Lift your knees off the floor and remain here for five to ten breaths.

Modify: Drop your knees to the floor but keep your head, back and hips in line and your abdomen drawn in.

GLUTE PLANK

Targets: Core, arms and the gluteus maximus.

Bike benefits: The glutes help power the down stroke and stabilise your legs.

Method: Perform high plank, and lift and lower one leg at a time, keeping your legs straight. Move slowly maintaining level hips. Repeat five times each side.

Modify: Perform your leg raises on all fours. Substitute forearm plank to keep the weight off the wrists.

FOREARM SIDE PLANK

Targets: Obliques.

Bike benefits: Strong obliques reduce side-to-side swaying, while gluteus medius stabilises your legs.

Method: Shift onto your side and stack your feet on top of each other as if standing. Position your elbow under your shoulder and spread your fingers. Raise your hips and lie the top arm down your side to add weight. Remain looking forwards. Stay for five to ten slow deep breaths. Alternatively, lift your hips on an inhalation and lower on an exhalation. Pulsing your hips like this challenges your lower obliques. Switch sides.

Modify: Weak core: Perform with the knees resting on the floor. Bend the legs into a 90-degree position and align the knees with the torso. Lift the hips.

GLUTE MEDIUS SIDE PLANK

Targets: Glute medius at the side of your buttocks.

Bike benefits: This smaller and lesser-known glute stablises your thigh bone, minimising rotation.

Method: Begin in forearm side plank position. On an inhalation raise the top leg off your lower leg. Remain here breathing steadily for five slow breaths. Alternatively, lift and lower, synchronising the movement with your breathing by inhaling up and exhaling down.

Modify: Lie on your side. Stack the legs on top of each other as with side plank. Raise and lower the top leg.

CYCLING PLANK

Targets: Abdominals and arms. Stretches your back and neck.

Bike benefits: Cycling plank mimics a sprint/aero tuck position to build targeted abdominal strength. It also eases out cycling tension in your back and neck extensors.

Method: Perform high plank. Inhale, and as you exhale, round your back, tuck your chin in and draw your right knee towards your nose. Pause for a second, drawing in your belly. As you inhale slowly come back into plank, placing your right foot down. Repeat on your left side and continue to move from side to side, synchronising the movements with your breath. Repeat five times on each side.

Modify: Perform a gentler version on all fours.

Oblique Variation: To target the obliques take your knee to the outside of your elbow, hover for a second, and return to plank.

MIXED CORE TECHNIQUES

CYCLING CRUNCH

Targets: TVA, rectus abdominis, shoulders and arms.

Bike benefits: This challenging kneeling-based pose, taught by Yoga Sports Science®, will build cycling-specific strength.

Method: Kneel and position your hands next to your knees. Press into the floor and round your back, releasing your head down. Now lift your knees off the floor so you are resting just on the front of your toes. Stay for five breaths, maintaining lift.

Modify: Problems kneeling: opt for a traditional 'crunch' by lying with your back on the floor and curling the bent legs into your abdomen.

Advance: Lift your knees higher by peeling more of your feet off the floor so you are resting lightly on your toes, then 'pulse' in the pose by squeezing knees closer into your abdomen on an inhale and lowering on an exhale.

REVERSE PLANK

Targets: Upper arm muscles (the deltoids and triceps), back glutes and hamstrings. Stretches the front of the body.

Bike benefits: This half strength/half stretch pose is not an abdominal exercise but is a great plank counter-pose. It also reverses the rounded position on the bike, providing a welcome stretch to the front of the body, including your shoulders, chest and hips. It shifts the focus away from the overworked quads to your hamstrings, for balanced leg strength.

Method: Sit with your legs stretched out in front. Take your hands behind you, fingers facing forward, and press into the floor. Now lift your hips in line with your torso and draw the soles of your feet down towards the floor. Tuck your chin in and gaze upwards, or lift your head and look forward. Don't tip your head back. Take up to five breaths, then slowly lower down. Make fists with your hands and rotate.

Modifications: Wrist injury: avoid this pose.

Boats, Crows and Curl Downs

BOAT POSE

Boat is classed as an abdominal exercise, and it will work the rectus abdominals, but it does challenge your hip flexors. The flexors (which include the psoas and illiacus) literally lift your leg every time you pedal, but if they are already sore from riding, pick plank as an alternative; or try the modified version, with your feet on the floor, as it will lessen your hip flexor load. Drop into a runner's lunge (see page 56) to stretch the flexors afterwards.

Targets: Rectus abdominis, lower back, hip flexors, along with quads, hamstrings and neck muscles.

Bike benefits: Creates a solid, stable core while working your hip flexors responsible for the repetitive leg lifting motion. Boat also improves balance.

Method: Sit with your feet on the floor, hip-distance apart. On an inhale raise both feet, keeping your legs bent. Lift your chest to prevent falling backwards. Take your arms parallel and spread your fingers. Look ahead and take five to ten slow, deep breaths.

Modifications: If your hip flexors are sore from cycling, avoid this pose, or keep your feet on the floor and lean back maintaining lift in your chest.

Advance: Straighten your legs (this requires supple hamstrings!), but only if your back doesn't round. Or extend one leg at a time. Raise your arms up parallel with the ears.

TWISTING BOAT

Targets: Obliques, rectus abdominis and hip flexors.

Bike benefits: The obliques 'still' your torso when cycling while strong, supple hip flexors raise each thigh.

Method: Perform boat with the hands interlinked behind the head. Inhale. As you exhale, rotate your torso to your right and move your knees to your left. Inhale back to the centre. Exhale and rotate your torso to the left and move the knees to the right. Maintain lift in your chest. Repeat five times each side.

Modify: If your hip flexors are already sore from cycling avoid this pose or keep your feet on the floor, lean back and twist. Keep your chest lifted.

Advance: Repeat, but with your hands interlocked behind your head.

CROW BALANCE

Targets: Abdominals and arms and improves balance. Good party trick!

Bike benefits: Crow replicates the cycling stance strengthening the muscles that brace your upper body over the handlebars. The core stabilises your torso just as it should on the bike.

Method: Crow takes practice, but don't be disheartened if you don't lift off the first few times as just the action of preparing for it works the core. To prepare, come into a squatting position on the balls of your feet. Place your arms just inside your knees and spread your palms on to the floor, shoulder-width apart. Draw your belly in and come high onto your toes, rounding your back and leaning weight into your hands. Raise your head and look up. Take care not to tip too far forwards, but when ready, press your

knees into your upper arms and lift your toes slowly off the floor. Stay for five breaths and lower down. Make fists with your hands and rotate.

Modify: Wrist injury: avoid this pose.

Advance: Over time, play with extending one leg behind you.

CURL DOWNS (AND CURL UPS)

Sometimes working slowly is more challenging, as is demonstrated by curl downs. This abdominal strengthener is also a good way to transition from sitting to lying without disrupting your yoga practice.

Targets: Rectus abdominis.

Bike benefits: Strong abs will counter highly developed back muscles from cycling.

Method: Sit with your legs stretched out in front, toes pointing to the ceiling. Straighten your arms and interlace your fingers. Tuck your chin in and begin to uncurl down to lying in slow motion,

1

2

keeping the breath flowing through your nose. Aim for a smooth, constant descent. Once down, reverse the process and curl up to sitting at the same slow, smooth pace. Repeat ten times resisting the urge to rush.

Locust

Locust is a great pose for cyclists as it strengthens the entire back of the body, including your hamstrings (which are often weaker than quads in cyclists), glutes and back muscles. Experiment with variations to focus on your power-providing glutes or to bolster your time trial position. Sit back on your heels periodically to stretch out your lower back.

BASIC LOCUST

Targets: Erector spinae, glutes and hamstrings.
Bike benefits: Locust is a great 'all-in-one' for cyclists. It strengthens the entire back of the body, including the extensor erector spinae. It also releases tension in your shoulders after hours spent rounded over the handlebars, especially with your hands clasped behind your back.

Method: Try your upper body first. Lie face downwards with your arms by your sides. On an inhale keep your legs grounded, but raise your torso and arms, spreading your fingers. Remain looking down. Stay for five slow breaths then lower down and sit back in extended child (see page 93). For a full locust, repeat, but raise both legs off the floor too.
Modify: Keep your legs on the floor.

BACK STRENGTH

AERO TUCK SEQUENCE

Holding the aero tuck position requires a combination of flexibility in your lower back, hips and hamstrings, resilient abs, and supreme upper body strength. This series, based on locust, is designed to help you sustain your lower posture required in a time trial or triathlon by strengthening all the muscles that stabilise the scapula or shoulder blades.

1 Locust: perform the basic locust as described on page 141. Repeat four times.

2 Locust 'T' arms: Bring your arms in line with your shoulders with your palms facing forwards. Inhale, raise your upper body, arms and legs, exhale and lower. Repeat four times.

3 Locust 'Y' arms: Bring your arms forward a little, so they form a Y shape, palms face down. Inhale, raise your upper body, arms and legs, exhale and lower. Repeat four times.

4 Locust 'W' arms: From the Y shape, bend your arms and draw your elbows back to make a W shape. Inhale, raise your upper body, exhale and lower. Repeat four times.

End by sitting slowly back on your heels in extended child.

Glute focus

The gluteals, or buttock muscles, are often left out of a strength and conditioning repertoire, but gluteus maximus performs a vital role kick-starting the 'down' phase of pedalling and provides the power to accelerate and climb hills. Strong glutes also help reinforce your lower back; a potentially weak spot for cyclists.

LOCUST LEGS

Targets: Gluteus maximus, hamstrings and lower back.
Bike benefits: The glutes provide the explosive boost required to speed up and ascend hills.
Method: Lie on your front with the forehead resting on the floor and bring your arms close by the sides, palms face down. Inhale and raise just your right leg off the floor, keeping your leg straight and your hips grounded and level.

Exhale and lower. Repeat three more times, moving from leg to leg. Rise slowly up to all fours and sit back on your heels.

GLUTE STOPWATCH TECHNIQUE

Targets: Gluteus maximus and hamstrings.
Bike benefit: This Yoga Sports Science® strengthening technique aims to isolate the glutes to focus in on these power-generating muscles.
Method: Lie on your front and place a stopwatch on the floor so that it is clearly in view. Bend your right leg and face the sole of your foot towards the ceiling. Rest on your forearms and turn on the stopwatch. Inhale and raise your right thigh off the floor without lifting your hip. Remain here, gazing at the stopwatch, for as long as you can. Try to relax the back of your leg (your hamstrings) as much as possible so that the glutes do the majority of the lifting work. Return your leg on an exhalation and switch legs. Rise slowly up to all fours and sit slowly back on your heels.

THE BRIDGE SERIES

Bridge is a fantastic all-rounder for cyclists; if you only have time for one pose, make it bridge. It strengthens your hamstrings to ensure they balance your quads. It also works the glutes and reinforces your back muscles. Like many yoga postures, it also has a dual stretching role. Bridge 'opens' the front of the body including the often tight chest, or pectoralis muscles. This backbend also releases tension, aids deep breathing and prevents that unwanted cycling by-product: rounded shoulders. Finally, it decompresses the back of your neck after hours on the road, holding your head up in extension.

BASIC BRIDGE

Targets: Gluteus maximus, quads and hamstrings. Stretches hip flexors, pectoralis muscles and shoulders.

Bike benefits: Gluteus maximus and your quads power your legs. Stretching the front of the body reverses the closed-in cycling stance thereby releasing tension in your chest, back and shoulders.

Method: Lie on your back with your legs bent and feet on the floor, hip-distance apart. Take your arms by the side, palms face down. On an inhale press your palms into the floor and raise your hips up. Ensure your knees stay aligned with your hips and don't sway out or inwards. Tuck your chin in. Stay for five, or more, breaths, maintaining lift. To exit and work the deep abdominals, ease down in slow motion and hug your legs into your abdomen.

HAMSTRING BRIDGE

Targets: Hamstrings, quads and glutes.

Bike benefits: Cyclists rely on their quads (at the front of the thigh). This can leave your hamstrings weaker in comparison. Strength at both the front and back of your thigh is required to maximise power in the pedal stroke.

Method: Prepare to perform basic bridge, but move your feet further away. On an inhale press your palms into the floor and raise your hips up. Ensure your knees stay aligned with your hips. Tuck your chin in. Stay for five breaths maintaining lift. To exit, and work the deep abdominals, ease down in slow motion and hug your legs into your abdomen.

CYCLING BRIDGE

Targets: Intensifies the work of the glutes and hamstrings.

Bike benefits: This bridge variation replicates the pedalling motion and forces your glutes to work in isolation.

Method: Perform bridge. Shift the weight onto your right foot and slowly raise your left leg off the floor, keeping it bent. Lower your foot gradually down and switch sides. Work slowly, shifting from foot to foot. Repeat five times each side. Ease down in slow motion and hug your legs into your abdomen.

Advance: Move slower, maintaining lift in your hips.

TWISTING CORE TECHNIQUES

Lying core twist

The lying core twists primarily work the obliques, but improve overall abdominal strength as the muscles work to control and slow the side-to-side leg movement. They are a good choice if you are tired post-ride as they don't require too much effort and they lead nicely onto recovery postures: simply loop a strap around your feet for a relaxing hamstring stretch, or bend your legs, rest them on the floor and relax into the twist. Finally, these rotations shift cyclists out of their forwards-only plane, thereby releasing shoulder, torso and hip tension.

LYING CORE TWIST 1

Targets: Obliques. Stretches your torso, hips and neck.
Bike benefits: The obliques reduce torso rotation. Twists move cyclists through other planes of motion to maintain a supple body.
Method: Lie on your back and hug your legs into your abdomen. Keep your legs here and extend your arms out, shoulder-height, palms facing up. Press your lower back into the floor and maintain this pressure throughout. Inhale, and on an exhalation sway both knees to your right. Hold them a few inches above the floor, then, as you inhale, ease them back to the centre. Repeat to your left side. Perform five times turning your head in the opposite direction to your knees to ease out tension from your neck and shoulders. End by hugging both legs into your abdomen and rocking from side to side.
Modify: Keep both feet on the floor, especially if you have lower back issues.

LYING CORE TWIST 2

This variation uses the weight of the top leg to increase the core work.

Perform lying core twist as before, ensuring your lower back is pressed firmly into the floor, but as you move both knees to one side straighten the top leg. Pause for a second keeping both legs off the floor. As you exhale tuck the top leg back in, draw your abdomen in and bring your legs back to the centre. Repeat to your left side. Perform five times turning your head in the opposite direction to your knees. Repeat on the other side. End by hugging both legs into your abdomen and rocking from side to side.

09

' With cycling you get into a stride, a rhythm, a continuous movement of pedalling and breathing. The same is said for faster styles of yoga where each pose transforms continuously into the next and the breath carries one forward. It calms and heals while increasing the heart rate and strengthening the core. I also find I consciously process the same issues on my yoga mat as I do in a race, and so – with a steady yoga practice – arrive much more mentally and physically ready at the start line. '

Kristen Gentilucci, Early Bird Women's Developmental Cycling Team, USA

So far the yoga postures in this book have been offered as static exercises, held still to either provide a deep, satisfying stretch or to strengthen the muscles isometrically. This is a sensible way to learn precision and technique, but, once mastered, athletes are often drawn to more energetic styles of yoga like vinyasa flow, power yoga or ashtanga, which weave these postures into faster-paced sequences. Up to half the students in these dynamic yoga classes may be male, and many are sportspeople looking for a more challenging route to flexibility than holding static stretches.

In a 'flow' the postures are linked using the breath, so the practitioner will inhale in one posture and exhale as they transition into the next. This concept of synchronising the breath and movement takes practice, but it's what distinguishes yoga from purely mechanical stretching or aerobics.

FAST-MOVING SEQUENCES

Eventually, synching breath and movement becomes automatic, and even meditative, as the mind latches onto its sound and rhythm, momentarily forgetting life's worries or distractions and gaining a clear focus. To reach this calm mental state it is essential to breathe through your nose. It will slow down the breath, giving you more time to transition between postures. Nasal breathing also encourages the body's relaxing and calming parasympathetic response so even if it is a challenging flow you still feel at ease.

The sequences in this chapter are split into two sections:

1 **Post-ride flows** comprise gentler sequences that ease tension out of the major cycling muscles, primarily your hamstrings, quads and hip flexors, but also the entire back and shoulders. Practise them immediately after cycling to keep the body supple and injury-free.
2 **Cyclist's strength flows** should be practised on non-riding days, and particularly off-season, when you are cycling less, in order to build up cycling-specific strength. Being whole-body exercises, they will correct muscular imbalances and create a strong, lean body, to keep you light on the bike.

In true yoga style, most of the strength flows also stretch. The ultimate flow is the cyclist's sun salutation. This is a sequence of stretching and strengthening poses based on the traditional Indian series of forward-bends and backbends, but with adaptations made to suit cyclists including more chest-opening and lower back-strengthening movements. Sun salutations are highly versatile, and this chapter will show you how to personalise yours by slotting in extra posture to loosen your hips, bolster your upper back or strengthen the glutes.

Please note: A degree of familiarity with the individual postures is required before attempting to link them in the following flowing sequences. All the postures – set here in bold type – are outlined in the previous chapters so please refer back for detailed instructions.

POST-RIDE FLOWS

Post-ride flows are less strenuous sequences practised straight after training when the muscles are still warm. Select one area to focus on, such as tight hips or shoulders, or perform the all-in-one stretch/strength sequence: the cyclist's sun salutation.

Standing stretch sequence

This standing sequence can be done anywhere – no mat required – making it ideal for outdoors, either after a ride or to release tightness, or when you stop for a break. It will restore length in your leg muscles, release both shoulder and back tension and improve balance.

Targets: Iliotibial band, hamstrings, quads, shoulders, back and neck.

1 Inhale: Stand with feet hip-distance apart. **Mountain pose.**

2 Exhale: Sweep your right arm up, cross your right leg over your left and side-bend to your left, sliding your left hand down your outer thigh. **Standing ITB stretch.**

3 Inhale: Back to the centre. **Mountain pose.**

4 Exhale: Sweep your left arm up, cross your left leg over your right and side-bend to your right, sliding your right hand down your outer thigh. **Standing ITB stretch.**

5 Inhale: Back to the centre. **Mountain pose.**

6 Shift your weight onto your left foot. Slowly bend your right leg and hug the leg into the abdomen with both hands. **Balancing leg hug. Hold for four breaths.

7 Slide both hands down to your foot and draw your leg back into a quad stretch. **Cyclist's Quad stretch. Hold for four breaths.

8 Inhale: Release your right foot to the floor. **Mountain pose.**

9 Exhale: Bend your knees and come into a forward-bend. Let the arms dangle or fold them. **Shoulder hang.**

10 Inhale: Release your arms, bend your knees and uncurl slowly up to standing. **Roll ups.**

11 Repeat the sequence from hugging the left leg in step 6.

Tight hips sequence

Many cyclists omit hip flexors from a stretching sequence, but these muscles at the top of your thigh lift your leg on each pedal stroke. Without adequate stretching they can get shorter and tighter, which can cause knock-on problems with your lower back. This sequence – based on runner's lunge – also stretches the groin, adductors (inner thighs) and muscles at the side of your hip. It is a slower flow to allow time for muscular release.

Targets: Hip flexors, quads, adductors and iliotibial band.

Hold each pose statically for four breaths.

1 Sink into a runner's lunge with the right leg in front. Hold for four breaths. **Runner's lunge.**

2 Draw your abdomen in and lift your upper body. Lean slightly back. Hold for four breaths. **Runner's lunge 2.**

3 Sweep your left arm up and over and side-bend to your right. Hold for four breaths. **Runner's lunge 3.**

4 Return to basic runner's lunge. **Runner's lunge 1.**

5 Lift your back knee off the floor. **Runner's lunge 4.**

6 Turn to the side with your fingertips still on the floor and turn your toes out so the legs are wide. Bend your left leg, shifting to your left so your right leg straightens. Bend the right leg so the left leg straightens. Shift from side to side, breathing steadily. **Low Side Lunges.**

7 Turn to your left to perform runner's lunge, left foot in front. **Repeat the sequence.**

Quad release sequence

This sequence revolves around the kneeling position, but if you find kneeling impossible or uncomfortable, opt for a standing quad stretch, or practise kneeling statically using padding (see Chapter 4).

1 Inhale: Rise up into a high kneeling position and take your arms wide, fingers spread. **Kneeling backbend.**

2 Exhale: Lower to a kneeling position. Place your palms on the floor behind you, fingers pointing away.

3 Inhale: Slide the right foot out, press your palms into the floor and lift your hips up to the ceiling. Hold for four breaths. **Half kneeling quad stretch.**

4 Exhale: Lower down and return to a kneeling position.

5 Inhale: Press your palms into the floor and lift your hips up to the ceiling. Hold for four breaths. **Full kneeling quad stretch.**

6 Exhale: Sink into **extended child pose** by bringing the forehead to the floor and resting your arms by the sides.

7 Repeat, sliding the left foot out in step 3.

Upper backache sequence

Nagging post-ride ache in your upper back? Remedy this with an upper backache and smaller neck stretch variation. For maximum release deepen the breathing and perform both in slow motion.

Targets: Pectoralis (chest muscles), rhomboid and trapezius (upper back) and shoulder muscles.

1 **Stand tall with your feet hip-width apart.** **Inhale:** Sweep your arms wide and spread your fingers. Raise your chin slightly. **Arms wide.**

2 **Exhale:** Cross your arms over your chest. Reach for your shoulder blades and round your back. Tuck your chin in. **Shoulder wrap.**

3 **Inhale:** Sweep your arms wide. **Arms wide.**

4 **Exhale:** Repeat Shoulder Wrap, crossing the other arm in front. **Shoulder wrap.**

5 **Inhale:** Sweep your arms wide. **Arms wide.**

6 **Exhale:** Cross your arms at your elbows and bring the palms together. Hold for four breaths. **Eagle arms.**

7 **Inhale:** Sweep your arms wide. **Arms wide.**

8 **Exhale:** Repeat Eagle arms but crossing the other arm in front. **Eagle arms.**

9 **Inhale:** Sweep the arms behind your back and interlock your fingers. **Shoulder opener.**

10 **Exhale:** Bend your knees deeply and tip forwards lifting your arms higher. Stay for four breaths. **Shoulder release.**

11 **Inhale:** Bend your knees more deeply, straighten your back, draw your abdomen in and rise up. **Mountain pose.**

12 Roll your shoulders. **Shoulder rolls.**

Neck stretch variation

Neck tension or headaches post-ride? Try this simple sequence either with the breath or hold each part statically for four breaths.

Targets: Neck extensors, rhomboids and trapezius.

1 **Sit or stand.** Interlock your fingers and take your hands behind your head. Keep your back straight. **Inhale:** Draw your elbows back. **Elbows back**.

2 **Exhale:** Tuck your chin in and draw your elbows together. **Extensor stretch**.

3 **Inhale:** Draw your elbows back. **Elbows back**.

4 **Exhale:** Tuck your chin in and draw your elbows together. **Extensor stretch**.

5 Slide your hands to your shoulders. Let the breath flow while you perform some slow motion shoulder rolls. **Shoulder rolls**.

6 Slide your arms by the sides and perform some slow head rolls. **Head rolls**.

Cyclist's sun salutation

A sun salutation is a self-contained stretching and strengthening sequence designed to create a powerful, yet pliable, body. It comprises a series of forward and backward bends repeated to gradually increase flexibility combined with strengthening poses, like plank and dog. The cyclist's version targets tight spots like your lower back, Achilles and hip flexors while strengthening the abdominals and upper back, both of which need to be super strong to maintain aerodynamic cycling form. Learn the basic salutation, then tailor to focus on the core, arms or upper body by mixing in suggested variations.

Targets: Chest (pectoralis muscles), lower and upper back, shoulders, hamstrings, hip flexors and calves. Strengthens abdominals, arms and back.

Repeat at least twice each side.

1 Inhale: Stand with your feet together and arms by the side. Lift from the crown of your head. **Inhale:** Sweep your arms out wide, shoulder-height and come into a standing backbend. Keep your tailbone tucked in. **Standing backbend.**

2 Exhale: Bend your knees and come slowly into a forward-bend. Drop your fingertips to the outside of your feet. **Standing forward-bend.**

3 Inhale: Rise up halfway, making a right angle of the body and sliding your hands to your knees. **90° stretch.**

4 Exhale: Step your left leg back into high runner's lunge. **Runner's Lunge 4.**

5 Inhale: Press your palms into the floor and step your right leg back into **high plank.**

6 Exhale: Bend your arms and lower slowly down to the floor keeping the body in line. **Low plank.**

7 Inhale: Extend your arms by your sides, palms face down. Raise your upper body, arms and legs. **Locust. Exhale:** Lower down from Locust. **Repeat twice.**

8 Inhale: Press your palms into the floor and lift your upper body into a backbend. **Cobra.**

9 **Exhale:** Keep your palms on the floor and sit slowly back onto your heels. **Extended child.** Stay for four breaths.

10 **Exhale:** Lift up into **dog.**

11 Stay for 4 breaths drawing one heel down and bending the other leg to stretch the calves and Achilles. Move from leg to leg. **Walking dog.**

12 **Inhale:** Look to your hands, bend your legs and step your left leg between your hands, returning to the high lunge. **Runner's Lunge 4.**

13 **Exhale:** Step your left leg up and perform a forward-bend. **Standing forward-bend.**

14 **Inhale:** Bend your knees and rise up to standing. Sweep your arms out shoulder-height. **Standing backbend.**

15 **Exhale:** Return your arms to the sides. **Mountain pose.**

16 **Repeat from stepping your right leg back in step 4.**

Adapting the salutation

Sun salutations are extremely versatile. Here's how you can add variations into stages of the flow to target particular areas of the body, or simply to keep it fresh.

1 **Core and arm strength:** pause in **plank**, step 5, and perform **glute plank, forearm plank, forearm side plank**. Alternatively, pause in **dog**, step 10 and perform **cycling plank** (all chapter 8).

2 **Upper body strength:** pause in **locust**, step 7, and add the aero tuck sequence, from Chapter 8.

3 **Tight mid-back and upper back:** pause in **high lunge**, step 4, and perform **twisting lunge** and **lunging backbend** (all chapter 7).

Low backache sequence

A tight lower back needs to be eased out slowly and gently so either work with the breath or hold each posture for four breaths.

Targets: Your lower back muscles.

1 Lie on your back with your legs bent, feet on the floor. **Inhale:** Lift your abdomen to the ceiling so your lower back arches but keep your buttocks on the floor. **Pelvic tilt.**

2 Exhale: Press your abdomen into the floor. **Pelvic tilt 2. Repeat twice.**

3 Inhale: Draw both legs into your abdomen. **Knee hug.**

4 Exhale: Rock slowly from side to side. **Low back massage.**

5 Inhale: Roll back to the centre. **Knee hug.**

6 Exhale: Slide your right leg down the floor. **Post-ride releaser.**

7 Inhale: Back to the centre. **Knee hug.**

8 Exhale: Take your arms out shoulder-height and lower your legs to the floor on your right side. Stay for four breaths. **Lying twist.**

9 Inhale: Back to the centre.

10 Exhale: Lower your legs to the floor on your left side. **Lying twist.**

11 Repeat, sliding the left leg down at Step 6.

STRENGTH FLOWS

The strength flows link the static postures from Chapters 7 and 8 (core and power yoga) in dynamic sequences that forge cycling-specific strength. These strength flows are tailored for cyclists by reinforcing areas a rider needs to maintain correct posture and avoid injury. These include your quads, hamstrings, glutes, lower and upper back, various layers of abdominals and arms. Most postures both strengthen and stretch, creating long, lean muscles – perfect for staying lightweight on the bike.

Quad strength flow

This sequence anchors your legs in the warrior 1 lunge while moving your upper body through a series of dynamic twists and backbends to release shoulder and torso tension. To advance the flow adopt a low, wide stance, deepen the breathing and move in slow motion.

Targets: Quads, hamstrings, arms and upper back. Stretches hip flexors, calves, shoulders and torso. Improves balance.

1 Begin by stepping your left leg back into a high lunge Turn your back foot slightly out. Place your hands on your hips. Look ahead. **Warrior 1.**

2 **Inhale:** Rise into the ball of your back foot, lean over the front leg and sweep your arms behind you like wings. **Flying lunge.**

3 **Exhale:** Remain where you are but sweep your arms forwards and parallel. **Leaning lunge.** Repeat four times.

4 **Inhale:** Drop your fingertips to the floor in a **runner's lunge**. **Exhale:** Sinking the hips.

5 **Inhale:** Sweep your right arm up to the ceiling. **Twisting lunge.**

6 **Exhale:** Return your right hand to the floor. **Runner's lunge.**

7 **Inhale:** Sweep your left arm up to the ceiling. **Twisting lunge.**

8 **Exhale:** Return your left arm to the floor. **Runner's lunge.**

9 **Inhale:** Lift your upper body. Sweep both arms up and interlace your fingers behind your head. Tuck your tailbone under. Draw the elbows back. Hold for ten breaths. **Lunging backbend.**

10 **Repeat, stepping the right leg back at step 1.**

Lower leg strength flow

This sequence strengthens the calves and muscles of the feet and ankles. Try not to rock forwards or backwards as you rise up and down.

Targets: Feet, ankles, calves and quads. Improves balance. To also strengthen your inner quads (often a weaker spot for cyclists) squeeze a block or cushion between your thighs throughout the sequence.

1 **Inhale:** Stand tall with your feet together and arms by the sides. Inhale: Rise slowly up onto the balls of your feet. **Calf raise**.

2 **Exhale:** Lower down. Repeat once.

3 **Inhale:** Rise up as before but sweep your arms up. **Calf raise, arms up**.

4 **Exhale:** Lower down, releasing your arms by the side. Repeat once.

5 **Inhale:** Rise up and raise your arms as before. **Calf raise, arms up**.

6 **Exhale:** Keep your arms raised and spread your fingers wide. Lower down, but bend your knees and perform a high squat. Hold for up to 10 breaths. **Chair pose**.

Post-ride lateral flow

Break out of the linear cycling stance with this lateral flow that both builds your inner thigh strength and opens your hips.

Targets: Hips, adductors, iliotibial band. Releases tension in the torso. Strengthens quads and inner thighs.

Begin this sequence in a wide stance by stepping the feet wide and turning the toes slightly out. Slide the hands down the legs so they rest on the thighs. Test your stance by bending your right leg: the knee should track in line with the second toe of the right foot. If the knee comes forward of the foot take your stance wider so that you can still glimpse your toes when lunging.

1 **Inhale:** Standing in a wide stance, feet slightly turned out.

2 **Exhale:** Shift your weight over to your right by bending your right leg and straightening your left. **Dynamic side lunge**.

3 **Inhale:** Back to the centre.

4 **Exhale:** Shift your weight over to your left by bending your left leg and straightening your right. **Dynamic side lunge**.

5 **Inhale:** back to the centre. Turn your left foot out and right foot in. Bend the front knee. Raise both arms up in line with your shoulders, palms face down. **Warrior 2**.

6 **Exhale:** Side-bend to your left, resting your left forearm on the front thigh and sweep your right arm up and over by the ear. **Side angle pose**.

7 **Inhale:** Rise back to **warrior 2**.

8 **Exhale:** Turn the front palm up and exhale into a backbend. **Reverse warrior**.

9 **Inhale:** Rise back to **warrior 2**.

10 **Exhale:** Straighten the front leg and side-bend again to your left. **Triangle**.

11 **Inhale:** Rise back to **warrior 2**.

12 Resume the wide stance start position.

13 **Repeat the sequence, turning the right foot out in step 5, warrior 2.**

Core sequence 1: sprint and climb power

This sequence primarily targets the corset-like transversus abdominis muscles that 'splint' the abdominal wall when climbing and sprinting. Most of the postures use abdominal 'crunch' mechanics, but also employ the glutes for added power. If your lower back is weak or injured, step rather than jump up to your hands.

Targets: Rectus abdominis, gluteus maximus and the muscles of your arms and shoulders.

1 Begin in **high plank** maintaining a line from your head to your heels.

2 Inhale: Raise your right leg up, keeping it straight. **Glute plank.**

3 Exhale: Lower it back down. **High plank.**

4 Inhale: Raise your left leg up, keeping it straight. **Glute plank.**

6 Inhale: Lift your hips up into **dog**.

7 Exhale: Bend your right leg, round your back and tuck your chin in. Draw your knee to your nose. **Cycling plank.**

8 Inhale: Return to **dog**.

9 Exhale: Bend your left leg, round your back, tuck your chin in. Draw your knee to your nose. **Cycling plank.**

11 Exhale: Rise back to **dog**.

12 Inhale: Look to your hands, bend the knees, sit back on your heels like a coiled spring.

13 Exhale: Jump – or step – up to the hands.

14 Inhale: Lower to a kneeling position and place your palms on the floor. **Cycling crunch 1.**

16 Inhale: Lower to kneeling, Sweep your hands behind your back and interlace your fingers. Draw your shoulders back. Hold for four breaths.

Core sequence 2: still and stable torso

This sequence bolsters the sides of your torso and hips by strengthening the obliques and glutes medius. These muscles combine forces to reduce sway and channel your energy into an economic, efficient pedalling motion.

Targets: Obliques, glutes medius.

5 **Exhale:** Lower it back down. **High plank**.

10 **Inhale:** Lower back to plank. **High plank**.

15 **Exhale:** Round your back and lift your knees, keeping your toes on the floor. Hold for four breaths, squeezing your knees into your abdomen. **Cycling Crunch 2**.

1 Begin lying on the side, resting your head on your upper arm. **Inhale:** Raise the top leg. **Modified Glute Medius Side Plank**.

3 **Inhale:** Rise up into **Forearm side plank**. Rest the top arm on the side of the body.

5 **Inhale:** Lift your hips back to plank. **Side plank**. Dip three times. **Exhale:** Return to **side plank**.

7 **Exhale:** Lower your leg. **Side plank**. Repeat three times.

2 **Exhale:** Lower. Repeat three times.

4 **Exhale:** Allow your hips to dip towards the floor.

6 **Inhale:** Raise the top leg. **Glute medius side plank**.

8 Sit back on your heels. **Extended child**. Repeat on the other side.

❛ You have to keep your chimp in the cage – your 'chimp' is your emotional side, and in a pressure situation you have to react with logic, not emotion. Develop a mantra like 'cool and calm' when you are in a good place, to reiterate to yourself when things get serious. You can practise something a million times – like a footballer with penalties – but when it comes to the crunch, you need to transform into a ruthless robot or you'll choke and miss your chance. ❜

Bradley Wiggins, Team Sky UK, Tour de France winner 2012, *The Sun*, July 2012

Mastery over the mind is essential in a tough, endurance sport like cycling – a fact well known to elite level riders. A concentrated mind is not agitated by emotions such as fear, plagued by doubt or swayed by the actions of other riders into making impulsive decisions.

Yet many cyclists will devote months to honing physical training and not a second to considering their state of mind. Your mind can be your best asset if controlled and used to your advantage. Find out how to transform it from enemy to ally using the range of yoga-based on and off-bike concentration techniques in this chapter.

CONCENTRATING THE MIND

Taming your monkey mind

Bradley Wiggins' representation of the mind as a naughty chimp that must be tamed is similar to what Buddhists call 'monkey mind', where the mind leaps rapidly from one thought to another like an agitated primate.

The monkey mind is restless, unsettled and indecisive, but perfectly normal. Psychologists estimate that the average person conducts a non-stop internal conversation with him/herself amounting to a staggering 300 words per minute.

This flow of random thoughts might be a normal state of mind, but it's an unwelcome distraction in a sport like cycling that demands a cool head to make quick decisions, especially during racing.

Mental training is about taking charge of the impulsive mind in two main ways. The first is to slow down the flow of thoughts to reduce anxiety and create a focused mindset. The second is to implant a single, powerful and positive thought to drown out any negative ones, and jump-start the physical effort just when the body is flagging.

This chapter contains an array of mental training exercises based on yoga techniques and adapted to cycling. With practice, they will help both calm a restless mind and reprogramme a negative one.

Channelling and harnessing our stream of thoughts is the underlying purpose of yoga. Though now valued as a physical exercise system in its own right, the postures originally existed purely to allow the student to sit within lotus with a straight back and meditate. In the words of Patañjali, an Indian writer on yoga from the third century BC, 'yoga is the settling of the mind into silence'.

Concentrating, not meditation

Anyone who has tried to meditate, even for a few seconds, will testify that is it extremely hard to 'silence' this barrage of thoughts. But it is possible to channel them in one single direction. This is concentration, rather than meditation.

A concentrated mind is a powerful asset for a cyclist. It is not agitated by emotion, nor by adrenaline, and not swayed by the actions of other riders into making impulsive decisions.

Moreover, a strong, focused mind can handle the sheer physical exhaustion that is fundamental to an endurance sport like cycling. Often, what sets elite cyclists apart, after all the hard physical training is done, is their superior mental power.

The ideal cycling mindset

When powerful lungs and strong legs are not enough, cycling success hinges on state of mind. Riders may put in 17 hours a week of physical training, but some coaches say that the sport is 50 per cent mental, while others put the figure at 80 per cent. The ideal cycling mindset is concentrated, motivated, confident and flexible. This type of mind also has the ability to control anxiety and emotions. The more skilled a rider becomes physically, the more important the mental side.

At the beginning stages, it is definitely the total physical development that is important. Later on you develop more mental concentration, mental preparation to maintain the physical capacity. Next you develop the spiritual.

Eddy Merckx (opposite),
legendary Belgian cyclist

Finding the right technique

People tend to fall roughly into three categories of learning: visual, audio or kinaesthetic (tactile or physical). It makes sense, therefore, to pick a mental training technique that suits your learning style. For example, do you find it easy to visualise? Do you respond to positive 'self-talk'? Or do you prefer a more physical method of mental training that could be executed on the bike? It's also useful to pinpoint your mental weakness in terms of cycling. For example, if you suffer from pre-race jitters then try a deep breathing technique, or a pre-race dummy run visualisation, to ensure that nerves don't disrupt the day's performance.

Sometimes self-doubt is an issue. Telling yourself 'I haven't trained enough, I'm going to do badly' becomes a self-fulfilling prophesy. Or admitting 'this is tough, my quads are burning' only serves to intensify the pain.

In this case, thinking positive with a mantra or longer affirmation may allow you to flip negative thoughts into super-charged, confident ones.

All of the techniques in this chapter – some of which have been shared by professional cyclists and sports psychologists – require perseverance. But in a sport that demands mental as well as physical toughness, it's worth asking yourself 'what am I thinking?'

FIGHTING TALK

Mental mantras: 'kill the hill!'

'Mantra' means 'sound instrument' in Sanskrit, and is a word or short phrase silently repeated over and over to switch the mind into a certain state. Athletes have used mantras, and their longer version, 'affirmations', for years. The most famous use of a mantra was that of Muhammad Ali, who famously proclaimed: 'I am the greatest!'

Cyclists use mantras as a motivational pep talk, or – like Wiggins – to remain 'cool and calm' in the peloton. Mantras can also be adapted as a race or ride progresses, from saying 'Smooth' going downhill, to 'Kill the hill' for climbing, or 'Go! Go! Go!' for an attack.

Silently repeating a mantra over and over will drown out internal distractions like self-doubt or physical exhaustion and external obstacles such as other riders, traffic and wind or rain. The principle is: think it to make it happen.

Mantra essentials

A mantra must be:

1 **In the present tense:** Use 'I am …' to jolt your focus into the here and now. Don't waste energy either over-analysing a past section of a ride or fretting about a possible future outcome.
2 **Personal:** Select a word or phrase that will strengthen your weakest area. If it's hill climbing, try 'Kill the hill!' or 'Strong and steady' as you climb. If you are tense, try: 'Relax and flow'.
3 **Positive:** Mantras are never negative. Embed positive instructions like 'Here to Win' or 'I love to climb' to reboot a flagging body and mind. You've done the physical training; don't let the mind drain your confidence.
4 **Active and energetic:** Boost energy levels with 'Sprint! Sprint! Sprint!' or 'Go! Go! Go!'

Affirmations: 'I'm strong and I'm ready'

Affirmations are usually longer than mantras, comprising a sentence rather than a word or two, but serve the same 'mental pep-talk' purpose. The slight difference is when you might use them. While a mantra is a quick-fix reminder to 'Ride strong', for example, an affirmation is a longer-term mission statement. It therefore requires a little more thought. Affirmations can even be specific to an event: 'I will ride this time trial in sub-30 minutes'.

Synchronising mantra with cadence

Cycling is a very rhythmic sport, and many cyclists find a few bars of music will play on a loop in their heads coinciding with their breathing or pedal cadence.

This internal soundtrack is useful for keeping the mind occupied and maintaining pace, but its unlikely to provide the motivational kick you need when the going gets tough.

While most mantras are short, punchy instructions, a longer one is perfect for timing with each cadence and breathing rhythm if the terrain is flat. For example, a longer, calming mantra is: 'Nice and easy, pedalling freely' while a more aggressive one shouts: 'Better, faster, stronger, longer!'

The benefits of synchronising mantra with cadence are many: you are not only keeping the mind on-track, but creating a relaxing breathing rhythm that will keep energy-sapping tension out of the whole body. The mantra/cadence technique also helps maintain a steady pace, making it a useful mental training method for time triallists.

VISUALISATION

Professional cyclists use visualisation in various ways. One is pre-race to do a virtual dummy run of the route or section of the route, such as a steep hill climb that is playing on their minds. Visualisation can also be used while riding (see the on-bike techniques on page 172) to negotiate the peloton, chase down another cyclist or fight pure physical exhaustion.

All are valid ways of taming the 'monkey', and thereby controlling the self-doubt, fear or lack of motivation that can undermine weeks of intense physical training.

Think you can't visualise?

It's true that 'visual' learners are likely to find it easier to conjure up mental pictures, but we all have the ability. Prop your bike against a wall and study it for a minute. Take in as much detail as possible, such as colour or branding. Now close your eyes and 'see' the bike in your mind's eye, either in one whole or in sections: you are visualising.

❝ Visualising success is an important step to becoming a superstar athlete. If you don't believe you can win then it will never happen. Get into the habit of visualising positive performances, even training rides. If you have 10 hill reps to do one day, take 5 minutes before the training ride to visualise yourself riding each hill rep and succeeding with all 10. My experience with visualisation was with the Elite Nationals in Christchurch which uses the Dyers Pass hill climb on each lap of the race. Dyers Pass is a 1.5 km, 4-minute effort and I was able to ride the whole climb in my head in real time (meaning it took me 4 minutes to climb the hill in my head). I practised climbing successfully in my head so that when it came to race day I knew what I was in for. I visualised the pain in my legs and the numbers on my computer. I knew the climb so well I could even tell you what gear I was in. ❞

Nick Rice, Team New Zealand Pro Cycling

Off-bike visualisation: the perfect ride

The purpose of this visualisation is to mentally rehearse a ride/race or particularly tricky part of a ride, such as a steep hill climb, to reduce stress and boost confidence.

By 'seeing' the ride while you are calm and relaxed you are taking control of the emotional or fearful side of the mind (the monkey) and creating your own positive scenario.

Find a quiet place and either sit with your back straight or lie down. Take five slow breaths, breathing in through your nose and blowing the exhalation slowly out through the mouth.

Recall a situation when you rode particularly well. Take time to remember every small detail of this scenario by bringing in all the senses. For example, if it was a great hill climb, listen for the rasping sound of your breath and whirring wheels, feel the wind on your body or the sun on your face. Remember the surge of adrenaline as you pass other riders, and the mixture of exhaustion and exhilaration as you reach the top.

Now hold on to these positive feelings and either picture yourself handling one challenging section, or see yourself spinning effortlessly through an entire race or ride. The moment a negative thought appears or you feel the body tighten with tension, stop and rewind. You control this internal movie so the minute it goes off-script (which it will), start again. Don't expect to visualise for long the first few times but, like all things, it improves with practice.

Some riders will repeat the visualisation every night leading up to a race. Others, like British track cyclist Sir Chris Hoy, visualise the perfect race, and how to react to unpredicted scenarios, just seconds before it starts, blocking out the screaming crowd and TV cameras. To remain centred and calm amid all that chaos demonstrates a high level of concentration. The only thing left to do after visualisation is to turn it into reality.

On-bike visualisation

BUNGEE CORDS AND FISHING RODS

Cyclists have many of their own personal visual tricks that use the power of the mind to increase speed. In the bungee cord visualisation the rider 'hooks' a lamp-post, tree or corner, then speeds up to propel themselves past it as if propelled by an imaginary bungee cord. Equally you might hook an imaginary fishing rod onto a rider ahead and spin faster to 'reel them in'. The theory behind both visualisations is that it is better to think about increasing forward momentum, where you are feeling aggressive, positive and in charge, than being chased which is reactionary, and therefore negative.

It can also be picked up during challenging phases of a longer endurance ride, such as a steep hill climb ('here he comes, and he's attacked the hill!') or a tricky corner ('nice and steady, he approaches the first bend…').

Its inventor is the Irish mental fitness trainer and cycling coach Alan Heary, who has worked with Olympic and Paralympic cyclists. Heary originally created the technique for a swimmer who was finding training laps tedious, but it's had a great response from cyclists. It's popular with those who like positive mantras, but are uncomfortable using a boastful one like 'I am strong/powerful.'

'Self-talk is an important element in creating mental toughness, but sometimes it's easier to do it if you feel like you are talking about someone else', explains Heary. 'So play around with it. This way you can approach a hill climb as if you were Contador.'

THE COMMENTARY TECHNIQUE

In the commentary technique the rider imagines himself as the focus of a running TV or radio commentary that plays in his ear and guides him through various stages of a race or training ride.

This combination of visualisation and self-talk is designed to help riders maintain concentration and think positive. The commentary can be used for the duration of a short race, such as a ten-mile time trial, to rein in a wandering mind and detract from aching quads.

THE STEAM TRAIN

The steam train technique is half visualisation and half breathing technique. It involves imagining your body and bike as a single mechanical unit and will suit those who find visualising challenging or prefer a more physical method that also trains the mind.

The rider imagines they are a train, or some other machine, and purses the lips to expel 'steam' as they exhale. This system of breath control has the bonus of forcing the cyclist to breathe slower. Expelling the breath slowly will kick-start a longer inhalation, thereby encouraging an overall deeper breathing pattern (this is particularly useful if you've exerted yourself, maybe climbing a hill, and are literally 'out of breath').

Mentally, the cyclist can play with the idea of releasing 'tiredness' or 'lactic acid' with the steam, and even breathe in 'energy' or 'fuel' for the machine. The variations are limitless. The beauty of the machine idea is that it can't get tired and is unaffected by negative thoughts or other gremlins that regularly plague human cyclists.

Ten techniques for pre-race nerves

A racing mind, 'butterflies' in the stomach and loss of appetite are common signs of pre-race nerves, and can sap vital energy, leaving you drained before the competition even starts. Here are some simple ways to remain positive and relaxed that you can apply to any stressful life situation. Experiment with combinations of techniques to find a sequence that suits you.

1 Count the breath – close your eyes. Inhale for three and exhale for four or inhale four, exhale five. Always make the exhalation one single count longer, as this relaxes mind and body.
2 Blow out the exhale – as above but purse the lips as if blowing air out of a straw. Imagine it as steam/tension leaving the body.
3 Visualise breathing in 'calm', 'energy', 'positivity', 'confidence' deep into your lungs, and exhale any 'stress' or 'tension' as above.
4 Silently or audibly repeat a calming mantra.
5 Roll your head – side to side, keeping your chin tucked in. Pause on one side, then the other.
6 Roll your shoulders – slowly, first one direction, then the other.
7 Sweep both arms up overhead as you inhale through your nose. Sweep them back and down, making an 'ahhhh!' sighing noise through the mouth that sounds like steam escaping.
8 Sit with your head dropped down breathing slowly through your nose. Listen to the sound of your breathing.
9 Picture a secure place where you feel comfortable. This might be alone on a favourite beach or a cosy family scene. Take time to conjure up a detailed picture using all the senses.
10 Visualise the ride if you are sufficiently calm (see off-bike visualisation on page 171) and, in your head, ride it perfectly.

CYCLING AND THE ZONE

Can cyclists enter 'the zone?'

The mystical 'zone' or state of 'flow' has been experienced by many athletes, although often glimpsed fleetingly just once or twice in their sporting career. Athletes in the zone report varying sensations of effortless ease, a sense of invincibility and are 100 per cent absorbed in the task at hand: a state of pure concentration.

Eight characteristics of the zone

1 **Challenge–skills balance:** feeling you are challenged, but you have the skills to succeed.

2 **Action and awareness merging:** a feeling of being 'one' with your actions. Otherwise described as a union of mind and body.

3 **Unambiguous feedback:** you know clearly how you are doing and what you need to do.

4 **Total concentration:** complete focus on the task at hand.

5 **Total control:** a sense of being able to do anything without feeling like you have to try.

6 **Lack of self-consciousness:** no worries, concerns, fears of failure or self-doubt.

7 **Time distortion:** a feeling that time speeds up or, more often, slows down.

8 **The 'autoletic' experience:** the experience was so enjoyable that it was its own reward.

The zone is a phenomenon that tends to be linked more to runners and is perhaps closely allied to the 'runner's high'. Maybe it is linked to the high levels of endorphins often released in running. But can cyclists experience the same euphoria?

Susan A. Jackson and Mihaly Csikszentmihalyi include the testimonial of an elite cyclist called 'Simon' in their book *Flow in Sports*. Simon experienced the zone while competing in the Tour de France finishing the race with a seven-kilometre climb and describes his experiences:

I was totally absorbed, 100 per cent; that was all that mattered in the whole existence. It just amazed me how I could maintain such high concentration for three hours. I'm used to having my mind wander, especially under pressure. My body felt great. Nothing, you feel like nothing can go wrong and there's nothing that will be able to stop you or get in your way. And you're ready to tackle anything, and you don't fear any possibility happening, and it's just exhilarating. Afterwards I couldn't come down, I was on a high. I felt like I wanted to go ride, ride up that hill again.

Most Tour de France riders would tell a far more gruelling tale. Some have argued that it's just not possible to block out the level of pain and suffering experienced in the Tour in order to reach the euphoric state of the zone. But are there ways to experience a sense of it?

Concentration: 'critical component' of the zone

Of the eight zone characteristics, one stands out. Jackson and Csikszentmihalyi state:

> ❝ *Concentration is a critical component and one of the characteristics of optimal experience mentioned most often. Learning to exclude irrelevant thoughts from consciousness and tune into the task at hand is a sign of a disciplined mind.* ❞

All of the techniques in this chapter will improve concentration, but in a sense the entire book is geared towards this single goal. For example, Chapter 3 features breathing techniques that use depth and rhythm to rein in a wandering mind. Chapter 11 explains the need to recharge the mind through relaxation or meditation to return stronger and fresher. Also, all of the physical postures release muscular tension, and that, in turn, calms and concentrates the mind.

One technique to gain a more concentrated mindset is to focus your attention on that precise moment. Jackson and Csikszentmihalyi dedicate a whole chapter of *Flow in Sport* to 'Focusing on the present'. In practical cycling terms it means being 100 per cent immersed in your cycling performance at that second – not fretting about a poor start 20 minutes earlier or worrying about the climb ahead.

British track cyclist Chris Hoy claimed he couldn't hear the crowds at the 2012 Olympics, despite their deafening roar, as all his mental energy was being channelled into each second of his race.

Of course, road cycling is a longer game – hours and days, rather than minutes and seconds. One method of anchoring the mind in road cycling might be to focus on one specific element of your cycling, such as pedal stroke efficiency. This might be:

- **Pedal stroke efficiency:** Are you pulling up as well as pushing down? Is the stroke fluid?
- **The noise of the bike:** Can you hear the wheels turning or the click of the gear changes?
- **Upper body tension:** Are your shoulders tight? Are your arms bent or locked straight? Are you gripping the handlebars?

Analyse this one detail of your cycling performance as if you were driving along beside yourself in the support car, armed with a pen and clipboard. When you feel the mind drifting, pick another subject. This objective monitoring process keeps concentration sharp, places you (and not your monkey mind) firmly in control and provides continual performance feedback.

The 1–10 Technique

A simple but effective way to maintain concentration is to count pedal strokes. Begin with the right foot and count 1 up to 10. Then switch immediately to the left foot and repeat the 1-10 count. Switch from foot to foot, keeping a continual and steady counting rhythm. The mind cannot wander while counting. This technique has the added benefit of helping to maintain pace. It also aids pedalling efficiency by ensuring you are not favouring one leg but applying equal force to both.

' As a two-time Olympian now working as a neuromuscular physical therapist I know that recovering properly is of the upmost importance. To stay on top of your game a good routine of stretching to ensure muscle elasticity, along with nutrition and staying well hydrated will ensure you get the best from your body. '

Ciarán Power, physical therapist and former professional road cyclist

Yoga for Cyclists has already explored elements of recovery, such as static stretching, in some detail. This chapter introduces 'restorative' yoga, and explores simple breathing, relaxation and meditation techniques that will recharge both body and mind.

What is restorative yoga? As opposed to strenuous, strength-building standing or core yoga poses, these postures are 'passive'. This means that they require no effort and are held for longer periods to both facilitate a deeper muscular release, and begin a mental wind down.

Recovery yoga involves engaging the 'rest and restore' parasympathetic nervous system: the polar opposite of the survival 'flight or flight' response with its sweaty palms and pounding heart, triggered by stress. The idea is to deliberately lower levels of arousal so the body can recover and repair.

This process, along with a healthy diet and plenty of sleep, is an essential (but often overlooked) element of training, although many top athletes take a total break for a few weeks during the off-season.

The body is not designed to operate on high alert for long periods of time and inadequate recovery time will adversely affect performance (see box on overtraining, page 183) and general health.

RESTORATIVE POSTURES

These postures slowly tease out muscular tightness, but provide many additional mind/body benefits. The wall inversion freshens up your legs, while the recovery backbend and twist aid deep breathing and all of them are relaxing. Perform them after a heavy ride, or when you need to sleep but the muscles are still twitchy or the mind alert.

Comfort is key: use as many props as required under knees or behind heads to allow the body to relax.

You will need:
- a large, rolled-up towel
- cushions or yoga blocks
- some wall space or a chair
- a blanket or warm layers
- time: each pose is held for one to five minutes.

Recovery backbend

Backbends literally reverse the unnatural hunched posture that riders adopt for hours at a time, making them an essential component of recovery yoga. They ease tension out of the entire back, stretch your chest muscles or pectorals, which become short and tight on the bike, and 'open' your shoulders facilitating deep breathing.

VERSION 1

Lay your rolled-up towel vertically on the floor or mat. Lie on the towel so that the bottom edge sits in the curve of your lower back. Ensure your head is on the towel with your chin tucked in. Place a smaller towel under your head if it is tipping back. Bend your legs and place your feet on the floor. Take your arms by the side, palms face up, or create a right angle shape. Stay for one to three minutes. Exit slowly by rolling onto one side, removing the towel and rolling back to hug your legs into your abdomen.

VERSION 2

For a deeper backbend move the towel horizontally and position yourself so that the towel is under your shoulder blades – not your lower back. Move your arms into a right angle shape, palms up. If there's discomfort in your lower back, revert to version 1. It is important to be comfortable and allow a muscular release to gain maximum benefit from this two-in-one backbend and relaxation.

The benefits of massage

Massage is not just for pro cyclists. While a daily rub-down from your personal soigneur may not be an option, a once-a-month session is a good investment.

Massage is said to increase circulation by pushing lactic acid and metabolic waste out of the muscles, although its exact benefits are still debated.

A regular massage session will, at the very least, provide an opportunity to tune into your body. Your massage therapist can pinpoint any areas with tightness or adhesions that may be susceptible to injury.

Massage also has similar stress-relieving benefits to those provided by a yoga relaxation. It lowers the blood pressure and provides a chance to rest body and mind.

Pick your massage time carefully, though, as it can temporarily cause your legs to feel heavy; not something you want just before a big ride or race. Ideally, find a sports masseur who knows cycling.

There are, of course, cheaper alternatives to a massage therapist, as long as you have no specific injuries that require a professional's expert touch. All you need is a couple of tennis balls, an old sock and a foam roller. To self-massage your upper back, push two tennis balls into the middle of a long sock and lie on it so that the balls lie either side of your spine. Begin rolling up and down at your lower back and work your way up the tight erector spinae alongside the vertebrae.

A foam roller is an effective way to self-massage your legs, if you can handle the pain. Place the roller just above your knee and lie on it, working upwards in strokes to break down tight quad muscles. For more agony shift onto your side with the roller under your thigh and move up and down the length of the iliotibial band from just above your knee to the top of your thigh.

Finally, squat on the roller so that it nestles in the middle of the glutes – move in a small circular motion to massage the piriformis.

Recovery forward-bend

Follow the backbend with this simple forward-bend, which doubles as an anti-insomnia technique if done sitting up in bed when sleep proves difficult. A gently rounded back allows the extensor and neck muscles a chance to release slowly after hours in contraction on the bike. Further break down back muscle tension by directing some deep inhalations into the back of your torso.

Simply sit with your legs bent and feet on the floor. Let your upper body relax onto your legs, resting your abdomen on your thighs, if it reaches. Let your head hang and arms fall where they are comfortable. Take a deep breath in and let the exhalation out slowly through the mouth, as if blowing out of a narrow straw. Close your mouth and resume slow nasal breathing.

Now start to direct your breathing into your back. As you inhale, feel your tight back muscles expanding as your ribcage widens. As you exhale, feel your muscles slide back into place. This will facilitate deeper breathing on the bike by allowing your back to expand when you breathe, even when riding on the drops (see back torso breathing, page 46).

Wall inversion

The ultimate treat for tired legs, this simple inversion drains the fluid that builds up in your lower legs. It also opens your chest, provides a gentle hamstring stretch and takes the pressure off your lower back. No wall space? Lie on your back and rest your lower legs on a chair.

Shuffle close to the wall, turn side on to it, lie down and slide your legs up the wall. If the hamstring stretch is too intense, move further away. Relax your legs completely. If they slide apart, tie a yoga belt or dressing gown belt loosely around your ankles to prevent slipping. Rest your arms by the sides, shoulder-height, palms face up. Or place your palms face down on your abdomen to combine the posture with some abdominal breathing.

Overtraining

Arnie Baker MD in *Bicycling Medicine* (Fireside Books, New York, 1998) asks the following question: 'One of my rules of thumb is this: when you look at the bike in the morning are you raring to get on it or do you groan inside about the workout you have set for yourself?'

According to Baker the symptoms of overtraining include the following:

- poor, non-restorative sleep
- mood disturbances, including anxiety, irritability, loss of enjoyment and sadness
- poor performance with the same (or increased) training
- vague or undefined physical complaints.

Overtraining is caused by a large hike in training volume or intensity or too little recovery, and sometimes a combination of both. Chemical changes include a rise in the levels of the stress hormone cortisol and reduction in testosterone and glycogen levels.

Avoid it by not increasing the frequency, duration or intensity of rides too quickly, by eating well and staying hydrated. Baker also suggests scheduling regular rest days, sleeping at least eight hours a night and meditating. Both simple meditations and relaxation techniques to encourage a good night's sleep are addressed in this chapter.

THE GOOD SLEEP GUIDE

Getting a minimum eight hours of good-quality sleep is crucial for recovery. But even if you are physically exhausted it can sometimes take time to switch off. An overactive mind not only stops you falling asleep but can also wake you up sporadically during the night. This means a disrupted sleep, which affects the following day's performance.

Yoga's many relaxation techniques, or 'yoga nidra' (literally 'yogic sleep'), are the answer to priming body and mind for a good night's rest. They work primarily by relaxing the muscles, often in a systematic way by moving around the body (toes, legs, abdomen, etc.). Relaxed muscles require less oxygen, so breathing naturally slows, the heart rate reduces and blood pressure drops. In this condition blood is not needed to power the muscles, so it flows to your abdomen to resume digestion as if you were sleeping. This is the parasympathetic 'rest and restore' nervous system in action.

Be warned: if you dislike being still your body or mind may rebel in relaxation and twitch and fidget. This agitation is common, but persevere, as, after a little practice, the initial stages of relaxation will trigger what is called the relaxation response. This is when the body automatically drops into a relaxed state, and this will happen faster the more you practise.

Once mastered, relaxation can be used in two ways:

- **Seated** – as a quick-fix method of lowering adrenaline levels enough to 100 per cent focus, maybe before a race or crucial work meeting.
- **Lying down** – as a deeply restorative recovery tool to aid sleep.

Experiment to see which relaxation technique suits you, from visualisation to a more systematic 'tense and release' exercise.

Relaxation 1: tense and release

The tense-release relaxation works on the principle that if a muscle is tightly contracted for a few seconds, it relaxes further when you release the hold. This is a good technique if you have had a late training session and the muscles are twitching even after stretching.

Prepare by taking four slow breaths through your nose.

1 **Feet:** On an inhale, flex your feet so your toes point up to the ceiling and your heels push forwards. Hold, then exhale and relax. Let your feet fall out to the sides.

2 **Legs:** On an inhale, press the backs of your knees into the floor/bed, engaging your leg muscles. As you exhale let your legs relax and become heavy.

3 **Buttocks:** On an inhale, clench your buttocks and hold. Exhale and soften.

4 **Abdomen:** Inhale and press your belly button into the floor/bed. Pause and then exhale and relax your abdomen.

5 **Chest:** On an inhale, arch your back, lifting the sternum to the ceiling. Hold. Exhale and release.

6 **Neck:** Inhale and raise your head off the floor and draw in your chin. Pause. Exhale and lower your head back down. Roll your head slowly side-to-side.

7 **Arms and hands:** As you inhale lock your elbows and make fists with your hands. Hold. Release on the out-breath.

8 **Face and jaw:** On an inhale, screw up the muscles of your face and clench the teeth. Pause. Exhale and soften.

Relaxation 2: sweeping the breath

This is an effective calming technique, a mini version of which can be done sitting or standing to lower stress levels.

Fix your attention on your toes. As you begin to inhale imagine you are 'sweeping' the breath up the body. Move from your toes to your knees, to your thighs, abdomen, chest and top of your head. Pause. As you exhale 'sweep' down again moving in reverse. Try to time the journey up and down the body precisely to coincide with the breathing, so you reach your head as the inhalation ends and arrive at your toes as you finish the exhalation. Once mastered, slow it down by spending a second or two at each anatomical landmark (knees, abdomen, etc.). If performing a sitting version fix your attention on the base of the spine and as you inhale imagine you are breathing up the length of the spine to the crown of the head. As you breathe out visualise breathing down the spine back to the base. Let the shoulders drop as you exhale.

Relaxation 3: lead legs relaxation

Combine mental imagery with the breath to create a feeling of physical heaviness. If your legs feel particularly fidgety after cycling, spend more time on them, creating a feeling of 'lead legs'.

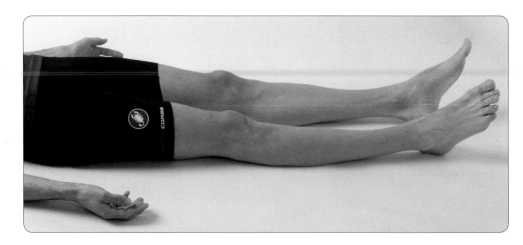

Repeat steps 1–8 of the tense and release relaxation, but this time concentrate on feelings of heaviness in each part of the body. For example, fix your attention on your head. Let the full weight of the heavy head sink into the pillow. Tell yourself about your 'heavy arms and leaden legs' pressing into the bed. Once you've worked from toes to head, it's important not to move as it breaks the 'spell' of heaviness – but if this happens, simply start again.

Relaxation 4: exhale the day

If the mind is buzzing and you need some mental clarity, pretend to exhale all the tension, stress or worry that has accumulated during the day. If you liked the on-bike visualisation techniques in Chapter 10, try this stress-relieving variation. It can also be done sitting to ease pre-race nerves.

Take a deep inhalation through your nose. Pause and visualise the negative element you would like to exhale (anxiety, tiredness, nerves, fear…). Picture it in as much detail as possible, then purse the lips as if breathing out through a narrow straw and slowly exhale the element. Visualise it leaving the body like steam and dispersing into the air. Repeat a few times until you feel the mind is a little calmer.

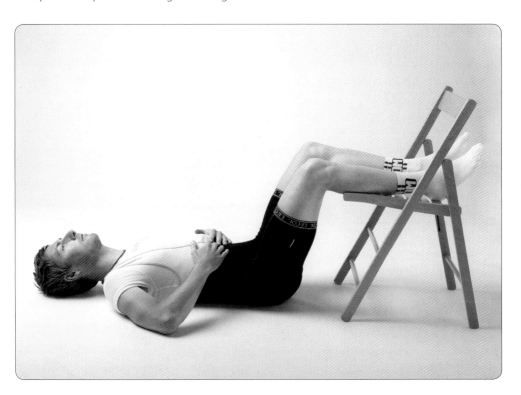

MEDITATION: MENTAL RECOVERY

We tend to think of recovery as a purely *physical* recovery, through stretching, massage, ice baths or diet, but a mind that is overloaded can disrupt sleep, cause stress and make it difficult to maintain a focused and alert state when cycling.

Don't be fazed by the word 'meditation'. If it triggers images of sitting in the lotus position, you are not alone. But this simple technique is really more concentration than meditation. Rather than trying to 'clear your mind' it provides a focus for the mind to latch onto: the breathing.

To put it simply, the breathing distracts the mind like a puppy with a bone, or a monkey with a banana. You are so busy monitoring it that the mind stops jumping from thought to thought and settles down. Once all these irrelevant, distracting thoughts have gone the mind is clearer and calmer.

Sit on a chair, or kneel or sit cross-legged on the floor. It's important to:

- **maintain a straight spine**
- **be comfortable**
- **be undisturbed.**

1 Take five deep breaths through your nose, making the exhalation slightly longer than the inhalation. On every out-breath let your shoulders release down a little, but maintain the straight spine. You can probably feel your abdomen or chest expanding as you breathe, and maybe hear the breath too.

2 Start to reduce the volume of air moving in and out so the breathing becomes less obvious and quieter. Stop 'deep breathing' and let the breathing settle into a more automatic, subtle pattern, just as if you were sitting relaxing.

3 Start to monitor the breathing in a detached way, as if you were making clinical observations. Watch how your chest or abdomen rises or expands as your lungs fill and empty. Are your shoulders moving up and down? Is the breathing slow or rapid?

4 Now narrow your attention onto the space between the nostrils, like a camera lens focusing. Watch the flow of air moving in and out. Can you feel the texture of the air? Is it warm? Does it make a sound? Are the nostrils flaring a little on every inhalation?

5 Continue to observe the breathing in a detached way. Try not to anticipate the next breath in or the next breath out. Notice the two pauses: one after the inhalation and one after the exhalation. Whenever the mind wanders (which it will) bring it back to this spot.

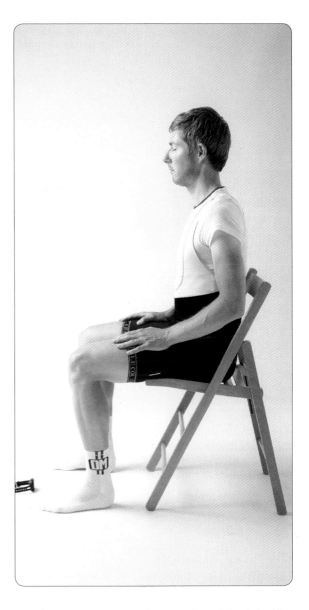

Stay for a minute or two to begin with, and slowly build up over time. If you want to monitor your progress, use a stopwatch. This meditation can be done anywhere. Once mastered in silence at home, try it on a crowded train using the power of your concentration skills to block out surrounding noises.

INDEX